IMAGES
of America

PEAKS ISLAND AND PORTLAND HARBOR

At the height of its turn-of-the-century popularity, Peaks Island had 18 hotels on the island, including the Peaks Island House, seen here around 1905. After the addition of the annex, the building in the background with the turret, the hotel could accommodate up to 600 guests. (Courtesy of the Fifth Maine Museum.)

ON THE COVER: In this c. 1890 photograph, spectators on the rocky back shore of Peaks Island follow sailboats racing across Casco Bay. (Courtesy of the Fifth Maine Museum.)

IMAGES
of America

PEAKS ISLAND AND PORTLAND HARBOR

Susan Hanley and Holly Hurd-Forsyth

ARCADIA
PUBLISHING

Published by Arcadia Publishing
Charleston, South Carolina

Printed in the United States of America

Library of Congress Control Number: 2021941926

For all general information, please contact Arcadia Publishing:
Telephone 843-853-2070
Fax 843-853-0044
E-mail sales@arcadiapublishing.com
For customer service and orders:
Toll-Free 1-888-313-2665

Visit us on the Internet at www.arcadiapublishing.com

*To my family, who do not completely understand my
interest in local history and support me nonetheless*
—SH

To Eric and Max, who listen patiently to my esoteric historical trivia
—HHF

CONTENTS

ACKNOWLEDGMENTS

The authors would like to thank the many islanders who generously shared their interest in and knowledge of Peaks Island's history, especially Reta Morrill and Judy Richardson, who helped in editing this book. The authors would also like to acknowledge the board of directors at the Fifth Maine Museum for granting permission to use many of the photographs in this book.

Unless otherwise noted, the images are all from the collection of the Fifth Maine Museum.

INTRODUCTION

Peaks Island's history as a seasonal destination began with the Wabanaki people who spent part of the year on the islands in Portland Harbor, hunting, fishing, and trading with one another. The Wabanaki enjoyed the islands for 13,000 years before Europeans began arriving, first to trade in the early 1500s and eventually to settle in the mid-17th century. Nearly 100 years of war, disease, and displacement pushed the Wabanaki farther north and west while the Europeans established permanent homes in what we now call Portland. By 1760, the English controlled the area and had settled on its surrounding islands.

In the earliest days of year-round settlement, just three families owned Peaks Island: the Bracketts and the Trotts (farmers) and Capt. John Waite (a mariner). During the 19th century, the population grew with an influx of families to support the island's growing fishing industry. Marriages brought still more inhabitants. During this period, the familiar island family names of Trefethen, Skillings, Welch, Jones, and Sterling arrived.

By the mid-19th century, Peaks Island became a vacation destination for urbanites who sought the fresh air and undeveloped landscape of the Maine coast. Steamships and railroads brought summer guests to Portland from New York, Boston, and Canada. They made their way out to the island on dozens of small ferries that arrived at multiple landings. Peaks Island went from having one hotel in 1850 to eighteen hotels in 1890 as islanders capitalized on the island's popularity. In a flurry of excitement, they built hotels, restaurants, shops, theaters, and an economy based on tourism.

The "season" was short. Tourist-based businesses had just three months to make their money, and competition was fierce. Whether visitors were from the local Portland area or from far away, they sought new and novel things to do while they were on the island. Islanders used the off-season to create the next big thing—balloon jumps, firework shows, a roller coaster, a zoo. Peaks Island earned the nickname "the Coney Island of Maine" and kept growing in popularity.

Some islanders turned their hand to property development, seizing on the opportunity to provide rusticators with campsites. Tents evolved into cabins as cottagers built summer homes they could come back to year after year, launching an island demographic that persists today—a population that combines year-round residents, summer cottagers, and day-trippers.

Shortly after the end of the Civil War, veterans began holding annual reunions on the island. Early reunion picnics were held at Greenwood Garden, Trefethen's Landing, or Evergreen. Later, veterans assembled for longer reunions in tent encampments. Eventually, the 5th Maine Regiment and the 8th Maine Regiment built permanent structures on the island, and happily, both survive to this day.

Ironically, prosperity in the 1920s led to the demise of Peaks Island's heyday. Rising wages gave the average American more disposable income, just in time to purchase Henry Ford's modestly priced automobiles. Vacationers headed inland, and Peaks Island grew quieter. The Great Depression, followed by a series of large fires, sounded the death knell for the Coney Island of Maine.

Left to its own devices, island life chugged along until the military arrived in 1942. The Peaks Island Military Reservation, built on land taken by eminent domain on the east side of the island, became home to 800 soldiers. The military built 58 structures on the island—batteries, lookout towers, barracks, mine casements, a mess hall, radar tower, recreation hall, and officer's club. Some survive today, including Battery Steele, albeit without its two 16-inch guns.

After the war, the island settled back into its quietude. The island's housing stock was cheap, and families across New England bought summer homes on Peaks Island during the 1950s and 1960s. The 1970s were marked by the arrival of new year-round residents, young families who found the island an idyllic and affordable place to raise their children. Many of the island's community institutions were founded during this time—the health center, the library, the day care. The newcomers helped reestablish the island as a thriving, year-round community.

Portland Harbor has always played an important role in Peaks Island's development, the backdrop against which the island's history has been written. The harbor has been a shipping hub since the 16th century. The city's motto, "Resurgam," Latin for "I will rise," alludes to Portland's repeated destruction and subsequent reconstruction. Again and again, the harbor's natural shelter and deep anchorage drew residents back to the area.

Given the frequent attacks on the city, fortifications were built to defend it from future assaults. Two forts were built in 1808 on either side of its entrance—Fort Scammell on House Island and Fort Preble in South Portland—to protect the main shipping channel into Portland Harbor. Both were active during the War of 1812. By the time Fort Gorges joined the harbor defenses in 1865, it was already obsolete. This familiar harbor landmark was never used in battle, and no troops were ever stationed there. But it is hard to imagine the harbor without it.

Lighthouses underscore the harbor's commercial importance. Ship captains protected their investment by choosing ports with lighthouse stations. By guiding ships into the harbor safely, Portland Harbor's lighthouses helped promote the transportation of goods and people. Spring Point Ledge Lighthouse and Portland Breakwater Light (affectionately called "Bug Light") both still keep ships from running on ledge, just as they did when they were built.

For the past 250 years, the island's fortunes have swung between times of prosperity and times of hardship. For residents today, things seem to have come full circle. Peaks Island is once again a tourist mecca that springs to life during the summer season, bursting at the seams with day-trippers and cottagers. In actuality, there are fewer boats coming to Peaks today than came at the turn of the 20th century. There are no giant hotels, no professional theaters, and no boardwalk attractions. Nonetheless, a carnival-like atmosphere fills the air as ferries come and go and the crowds disembark, ready to explore Peaks Island.

One

FERRIES AND LANDINGS

When Casco Bay Lines bought the *Sabino* in 1935, she had already led a storied life. Christened the *Tourist* in 1908, she ran out of South Bristol, Maine, before sinking in the Damariscotta River in 1918. Serving Peaks Island until 1958, she was retired and sold several times before arriving at the Mystic Seaport Museum in 1970, where she is still in use.

Portland, Me. Custom House Wharf. Casco Bay & Harpswell Lines.

During the late 19th and early 20th centuries, Peaks Island was served by several ferry lines. The early steamships were quiet, well-appointed, and large; some of them transported 1,000 people per trip. Casco Bay Lines emerged in 1919, a reincarnation of the cash-strapped Casco Bay and Harpswell Steamboat Company, itself the result of the 1907 merger of the Harpswell Steamboat Company and the Casco Bay Steamboat Company. The company added smaller passenger boats during the 1920s to improve the financial viability of year-round service. By 1959, the all-white fleet of wooden steamers moored at Custom House Wharf (above) gave way to the brightly colored fleet of steel diesel boats. In 1988, Casco Bay Lines moved to the Maine State Pier where a new ferry terminal building was constructed in 2014. (Above, courtesy of Susan Hanley.)

The *Forest City* side-wheeler was one of the first steamers to service Peaks Island. Built as the *Gazelle* in 1865 and used to transport summer tourists to Peaks Island, it caught fire at its winter mooring in Portland in 1883. The Forest City Steamboat Company used the $9,000 insurance money to lengthen and rebuild the boat and renamed it the *Forest City* upon its return in 1884.

Since the advent of regular ferry service, most visitors have arrived on Peaks Island at Forest City Landing, seen here around 1910. Vehicle ferries used the iron transfer bridge (right), and visitors stepped off the passenger boats on the opposite side of the wharf, greeted by restaurants and shops. Fares were just 5¢ each way. (Courtesy of Susan Hanley.)

The 1896 arrival of the stately passenger steamer *Pilgrim* ushered out the tired *Forest City*, which was sold shortly thereafter. The former Lake Erie steamer boasted a fine interior and a legal capacity of 1,100 people spread across three full decks. During the high season (July and August), the steamboat brought tourists out to Peaks Island 12 times a day. Because of her huge size, she was not used in the off-season. The Casco Bay Steamboat Company owned the Gem Theater, and theatergoers could purchase a combination ticket—round-trip fare on the *Pilgrim* and admission to the show—for just 25¢. Until she was retired in 1931, the company also used the grand *Pilgrim* for charter cruises, including popular "Sunday Sails," in which the boat traveled 40 miles among the Casco Bay islands. Bands and orchestras made charter excursions lively. Newspaper articles at the time advertised that Chandler's Band, established in 1833, would be playing during the cruise. The band remains active today (188 years later) under its current name, Chandler's Military Concert Band.

The steel-hulled *Machigonne* (above) was built and sailed from Philadelphia in 1907 to become the flagship of the Harpswell Steamboat Company. She was outsized, rated at 425 tons and 1,000 passengers. The interior (below) was luxurious by steamboat standards: airy cabins, plush seating, and carpets throughout. But the arrival of the *Machigonne* was the company's undoing. With overages she cost almost $95,000 to build, rarely ran at capacity, and forced repeated wharf repairs when she came in hard. After her first season, the Harpswell Steamboat Company faced bankruptcy. In 1913, after just six seasons in Casco Bay, the *Machigonne* was sold to a Boston company. After being requisitioned by the Navy during World War I, she returned to civilian life to ferry newly arrived immigrants from Ellis Island to New York City. She ended her career running between Providence and Block Island in Rhode Island, first as the *Block Island* and then as the diesel-powered *Yankee*, until 1979. (Both, courtesy of Susan Hanley.)

This view of Forest City Landing highlights the steel transfer bridge built in 1908 to accommodate the *Swampscott* car ferry. Vehicle transport aboard the *Swampscott* was primarily for the benefit of tourists. According to the 1908 State of Maine Automobile Register, there were 2,238 cars in Maine, but not a single one belonged to an islander. Notice the automobile in the center of the photograph driving toward the ferry. (Courtesy of Susan Hanley.)

Portland, Maine. Trefethens Landing, Peaks Island.

Soon after the Trefethens arrived on Peaks Island in 1843, they built a wharf that was long enough to reach deep water and bent to avoid a local sandbar. Trefethen's Landing became one of the island's main wharves but its length made it vulnerable to storms. By 1960, after repeated cycles of storm damage and repair, the Public Utilities Commission (PUC) condemned it as unsafe and closed it permanently.

14

Evergreen Landing felt more remote than the other landings. In the late 1800s, it was first enjoyed by "rusticators" who camped in the area, then by "cottagers" who built small summer homes around the landing. Evergreen remained undeveloped despite daily ferry service. The Davies sisters, summer residents, were influential in preserving the natural beauty of the area. Daughters of a wealthy Portland businessman, Mabel and Mary Davies created a manicured woodland walk on their Evergreen property that they happily shared with visitors. Removing the tangled undergrowth allowed the indigenous flowers to flourish among the rocks and pines. Both women were passionate about birding. Mabel's other passion project was advocating for prison reform in Maine. She testified before the legislature and visited jails in England, Switzerland, and France to see conditions there. Her sanctuary on Peaks Island provided respite. Evergreen Landing remained in use but was poorly maintained. It was damaged in a succession of storms, including two strong hurricanes in 1954, and was permanently closed by the PUC in 1960.

PEAKS ISLAND FERRY.   105

The *Swampscott* was purchased from the Boston, Revere Beach & Lynn Railroad by Edgar Rounds as part of his Island Ferry Company fleet in 1908. The double-ended ferry brought "twenty touring cars . . . some to remain for the season" when it arrived. Since she was painted green, a newspaper reporter likened her to a "giant water beetle" scuttling back and forth between Peaks and Portland. After 26 years plying Casco Bay, her hull layered with steel patches, the *Swampscott* limped into the car ferry slip at Forest City Landing and foundered. The four coal trucks she was carrying at the time just managed to drive off before she sank. Edgar Rounds vowed to salvage her, but in the end, she was scrapped for $235.

This undated photograph of the crew of the *Swampscott* includes the captain, purser, and deckhands. Steamboats also had an engineer, who ran the engine, and a fireman, who stoked the boiler with coal to produce steam. Crewing a steamboat was dangerous work as this 1903 account reveals. "As the steamer was approaching her dock at Peaks Island, Charles Hendricksen, a deckhand, while removing the forward gangway rail, fell overboard and was drowned." Riding ferries as a passenger was often dangerous as well. Boats sometimes ran aground or into each other in the fog. The *Swampscott* ran into a motorboat in Portland Harbor in 1909, resulting in passenger injuries. Inconvenience was another cross that islanders had to bear. In the early 1920s, Edgar Rounds stopped running the *Swampscott* as soon as the summer residents departed. Year-round island residents appealed to the city councilors to intervene, but Rounds refused to run his ferry unless he was allowed to raise the fares, and he threatened to sue the city if they granted ferry slip rights to a competitor. In the end, prices were raised.

The steamer *Greenwood* sailed on Sebec Lake in northern Maine until October 1886, when it was purchased by Freeman Weeks to bring tourists directly to Greenwood Garden where they disembarked on a dock just below the grounds. The 25¢ fare included admission to Greenwood Garden, but the steamer could also be chartered for sailing parties. Advertisements in 1888 touted the steamer's new feature—"lighted by electric lights." (Courtesy of Susan Hanley.)

The 500-passenger *Aucocisco*, shown backing away from the dock, was built in Portland and launched in 1897 for the Harpswell Steamboat Company. She ferried passengers around Casco Bay continuously until 1952, except during World War II. In 1942, the US Navy took over the steamship, painted her gray, changed her name to the USS *Green Island*, and used her to ferry sailors to and from naval vessels anchored in Casco Bay.

The steamer *Forest Queen* was built in 1887 in Athens, New York, for the Forest City Steamboat Company. Used as an excursion boat during the summer, she was frequently chartered for special trips around Casco Bay—going north to Bath, Maine, or south to Old Orchard Beach, Maine. While other steamers tied up for the off-season, the *Forest Queen* ran the island route in the winter.

The *Tourist* sails toward the Maine Wharf, where the Randall & McAllister Coal Company building can be seen to the left of this photograph. The *Tourist* was built in 1913 in Boothbay Harbor, Maine, but after more than 40 years in service, she was stripped of anything valuable and burned to the waterline at the Falmouth Foreside mudflats in July 1934.

From left to right, Mabel Babcock, Edna Davis, and Florence Ventres pose at Jones Landing in October 1947. At the time, Jones Landing was used for both passenger and car ferries. Jones Landing was named for William T. Jones, who originally ran a cooper business above the wharf before he died suddenly in 1880. Jones is credited with starting the tourist trade by converting his cooper shop into one of the island's first hotels in 1860.

A passenger ferry approaches Jones Landing, one of the oldest landings on Peaks Island. William T. Jones bought the land in 1849. During the early 1960s, as the Forest City Landing became increasingly unsafe, Casco Bay Lines rented Jones Landing from then owner Abraham Comfort of Florida. Jones Landing fell back into private use after Forest City Landing was rebuilt in 1966.

Swimming from the wharves and floats around Peaks Island is a centuries-old pastime. Although the dock in this 1937 photograph is labeled "Forest City Landing," it may be Jones Landing, located just north of the Forest City Landing. The Coronado-Union Hotel, which would have been behind the dock, had already burned down in 1918, and the great fire of 1936 wiped out other buildings across the front of the island. (Courtesy of Susan Hanley.)

A bustling Forest City Landing has both the *Nancy Helen* car ferry and an unidentified passenger ferry arriving at the same time, around 1940. Businesses on the landing itself included Ma Watson's restaurant, the ferry ticket office, and an ice-cream stand. A fish market can be seen perched on a slice of land beside Welch Street.

The *Nancy Helen* was a steel-hulled car ferry that joined the Casco Bay Lines fleet in 1936. The owner, Leon Herman, named the ferry after his granddaughter, Nancy Helen Cohen, who broke a bottle of champagne against the bow when she was just four, christening the new boat at Brown's Wharf in Portland. The diesel engine routinely achieved the dizzying speed of 16 minutes slip-to-slip, a marvel compared to the *Swampscott* that she replaced. The marvel was short-lived. A fire that started in the passenger cabin severely damaged the 114-foot boat in April 1941 while she was docked at her Peaks Island slip. Herman estimated the loss at $2,000. (Both, courtesy of Susan Hanley.)

Peaks Island was left without a car ferry after the *Nancy Helen* burned until Samuel Howard bought the *Narmada* in June 1946 and began running a private car ferry service with six daily runs between Portland Pier and Jones Landing on Peaks Island. Casco Bay Lines bought the 54-foot boat from Howard a year later and expanded the route to include other Casco Bay islands by request. Drivers had to back down the ramp to board the vessel on the Portland side, a real challenge for large vehicles with small back windows and no power steering. Although it only had a capacity of four or five cars, Casco Bay Lines used the *Narmada* until about 1955. When the *Berkley* arrived from Virginia in 1954, the *Narmada* was used exclusively for down-the-bay trips.

The *Berkley* was built in 1935, but it did not make its maiden voyage as a Casco Bay Lines vessel until August 27, 1954. The car ferry cost in excess of $60,000 and required pier upgrades that cost an additional $13,000. But with a capacity of 150 passengers and 8 cars, it was a significant improvement over the *Narmada*. Passengers enjoyed leather cushion seats, and cars had plenty of deck space.

Captains never had to turn the *Berkley* around, since it had two wheels on opposite ends of the wheelhouse and could be driven in either direction. An engineer worked below deck where a signal bell relayed the captain's driving orders. Driving cars onto Jones Wharf at Peaks Island was a challenge, and many cars scraped their bumpers on the steep ramp when it was low tide. (Courtesy of Susan Hanley.)

The 61-foot *Yankee Clipper*, built in 1958, worked at Sanibel Island, Florida, until she was sold to Casco Bay Lines in October 1964 and renamed the *Rebel*. With a 10-car capacity and no need for an engineer below deck, management labeled the *Rebel* "more efficient." Islanders did not necessarily agree since the boat's upper cabin could only carry 15 passengers. Another quirk was that with an off-center wheelhouse, the ferry leaned to one side when the car deck was not full.

The People's Ferry Company was incorporated in 1903 by Edgar Rounds of Portland. Rounds dabbled in everything—politics, business, utilities, and entertainment. But he was a bit of a chancer, squelching competition through the courts and legislation. In this 1929 timetable advertisement, he encourages automobile tourism and crowds of visitors—something today's islanders worry about. (Courtesy of Susan Hanley.)

John Allen, shown here at age 17 in 1925, was a ferry ticket agent at Trefethen's Landing. Allen could see approaching boats from home and then run to the dock to sell tickets for trips down the bay or up to Portland. He occasionally worked as a deckhand, staying overnight on the ferry and returning to Peaks Island in the morning, braving the boat's other passengers—rats and bedbugs.

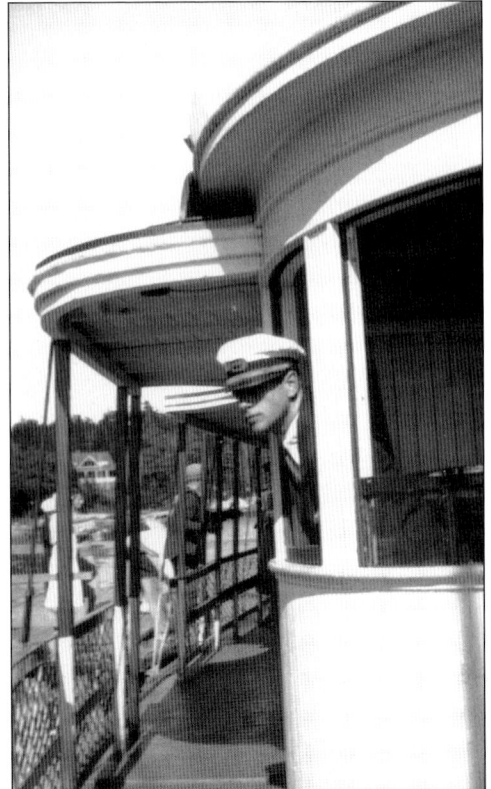

Captain Randall is at the helm of the Sabino on a clear day. Navigating Casco Bay during the age of steamboats was not simple. Before boats were outfitted with radar and depth-finders, captains navigated by counting the minutes and seconds between known points on the trip. Bells were installed on the wharves and rung to guide the boats in during fog and dark. Many a boat ran aground when a captain "lost his time."

THE EMITA - CASCO BAY LINES, PORTLAND, MAINE   2908

The wooden steamer *Emita* was built in 1880. In the spring of 1894, she was pulled out of the water so that the entire hull could be re-planked to repair the damage done by severe winter ice. She was converted to diesel in 1928 and ran almost daily until her retirement in 1953, when her engine was salvaged and her hull was towed to the mudflats near Salisbury, Massachusetts. She was burned to the waterline in 1961.

Passengers on the *Emita* could enjoy riding in deck chairs or standing at the rails on the upper deck. Either way, cool ocean breezes and scenic views brightened the trip. During inclement weather, passengers opted for comfortable, plush seats inside. Starting off as a pleasure craft that took tourists to Greenwood Garden and other island destinations, the *Emita* became the commuter and school boat during the 1940s and 1950s.

The *Island Romance*, seen here in dry dock, was built by Blount Boats of Warwick, Rhode Island, in 1973. It came to Peaks Island as the last in a series of new boats, the *Island Holiday* having previously arrived in 1967 and the *Island Adventure* in 1968. The three boats were the core of the Casco Bay Lines fleet during the 1970s and 1980s. Casco Bay Lines sold the *Island Romance* to El Dorado Cruises in Staten Island, New York, in 2014, where disagreements over the cost of boat repairs have kept it tied up and mired in litigation almost ever since. Casco Bay Lines hauls each of its ferries out of the water every two years for a complete US Coast Guard hull inspection and regular maintenance. While the boats are out of the water, hulls are repainted with a special paint that prevents corrosion, upper decks are given a face-lift, and propulsion systems are examined. In 1976, the red, yellow, and black fleet was repainted in red, white, and blue to commemorate the country's bicentennial. (Courtesy of Susan Hanley.)

The *Abenaki*, built in 1963, was the precursor to the very similar *Island Romance*, *Island Adventure*, and *Island Holiday* boats. One distinct difference was the large, open prow that became a playground for many island children when it was not being used to carry large items of freight. The *Abenaki* was even used to transport cars to islands down the bay by driving them into the boat's cavernous bow.

The *Island Holiday* cuts through an ice-strewn bay in 2003. During the early 20th century, when there were fewer boat trips each day, particularly cold winters resulted in ice-locked islands. Casco Bay rarely freezes over now due to year-round boat traffic. Most recently, the winter of 2014 produced overnight ice that the ferry boats had to break through in the morning.

The wide wharf at Evergreen Landing easily accommodated the crowds of people and tons of freight that arrived off the boats. The small house in the foreground served as a shelter for waiting passengers as well as the ticket agent during bad weather. Many of the cottages seen in the background are still used today.

The Trefethens built the first landing on the shorefront of their property before 1860; it may have been there as early as 1844, when the Trefethen homestead was built. This early-20th-century version has been widened dramatically at its endpoint so that crowds could disembark from steamers and travel to hotels in waiting horse-drawn carriages.

30

Two

Cottages and Families

The Bandbox Cottage on Prince Avenue was constructed around 1910, at the height of Peaks Island's "building boom." Almost 700 homes were built on Peaks between 1880 and 1930, most of them seasonal cottages that were only occupied during the warmer months. This cottage, also known as the Three Twins, was owned by Albert S. Ventres.

CAMP CASCO

PEAKS ISLAND.

1887

Camping in "wall tents" was popular on the island in the 1880s. They were comfortably furnished and often erected on wooden platforms, keeping occupants warm and dry. People who worked in Portland would spend their summer evenings in these tent camps—an affordable vacation for people who did not get a lot of time off. An article in a June 1887 issue of the *Portland Daily Press* reported that the campers were "composed principally of business men and their families. There are also a number of young men, clerks and mechanics, who make their home on the island nights. . . . Camp Casco has ten young men." An estimated 300–500 people would camp on the island during the summer season. As more boardinghouses and hotels opened, camping became a less popular option. Some people built cottages on top of the leftover tent platforms. (Courtesy of the Maine Historical Society.)

Among the most popular views from Peaks Island are Whitehead Passage and the famous Whitehead Cliffs on the eastern end of Cushing Island. These cliffs rise over 100 feet straight out of the ocean and are one of the highest points in Casco Bay. They were a trendy subject for landscape painters and photographers to capture. Here, they provide a scenic backdrop for an unidentified woman, possibly a member of the Ross family.

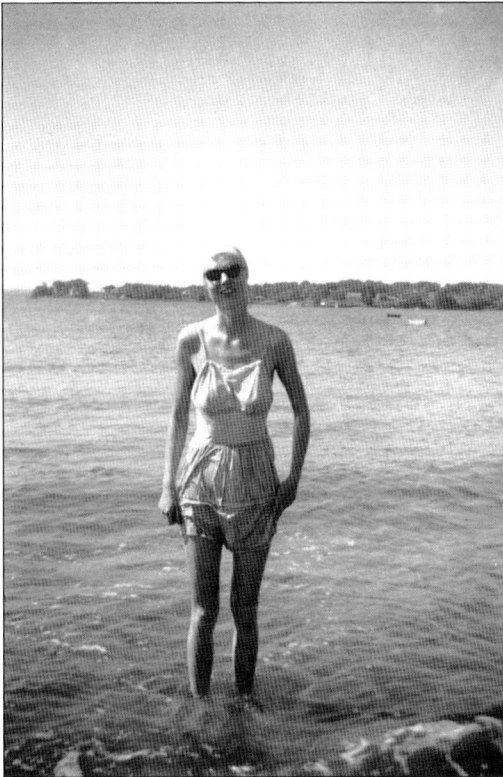

Florence Jenkins Ventres (1892–1965) is on the beach. Ventres was a teacher before her marriage. She raised two children living on and visiting Peaks Island: Albert and Mary. Florence was born in landlocked Colorado, but she clearly enjoyed the ocean. Her family photographs are filled with similar scenes.

Grand View Cottage was built around 1899 near Evergreen Landing, the northernmost neighborhood on Peaks Island. Evergreen was known for peace and quiet, its rocky, spruce-filled landscape far from the hustle and bustle of Greenwood Garden and Forest City Landing, what is now called "Down Front." Despite its seclusion, Evergreen had its own ferry landing at the time, making it a convenient destination to travel to. This cottage was advertised in local newspapers such as the *Casco Bay Breeze* and rented out by visitors to the island, sometimes for the entire summer season.

Seen here is a close-up of the porch of Grand View Cottage in the Evergreen section of Peaks Island. The couple is unidentified. Most seasonal cottages had at least one porch or other covered outdoor space so guests could make the most of their vacation, despite the weather. The Grand View Cottage porch is well-furnished with rocking chairs, wicker furniture, throw rugs, and a hammock. The little private island called Pumpkin Knob is visible in Hussey Sound in the background. Grand View was owned by Alice, K.B., and Helen Doherty in 1924.

Albert Smith Ventres, born in 1868 in Massachusetts, prepares a "shore dinner" around 1910. Clambakes and shore dinners were all the rage on Peaks Island at the turn of the 20th century. Some clambakes were small and fed just a few families, but commercial clambakes could feed hundreds of people at a time. A pit was dug into the sand that was then lined with rocks. A wood fire was lit to heat the rocks red hot. The rocks retained their heat even after the fire was extinguished. Clams, lobsters, mussels, fresh corn, and new potatoes were layered with seaweed and steamed for several hours. Ventres, an accountant who worked in Portland, owned several cottages on Peaks where his family spent a lot of their time.

A large group of people enjoy a classic shore dinner al fresco. Lobsters and potatoes, Maine's signature foods, are visible on the diners' plates. They have the luxury of sitting at a table rather than eating out of their laps. Lobster was once so abundant it was considered a "trash" food, but by 1900, it was a delicacy, and tourists would seek it out on their vacations to Maine.

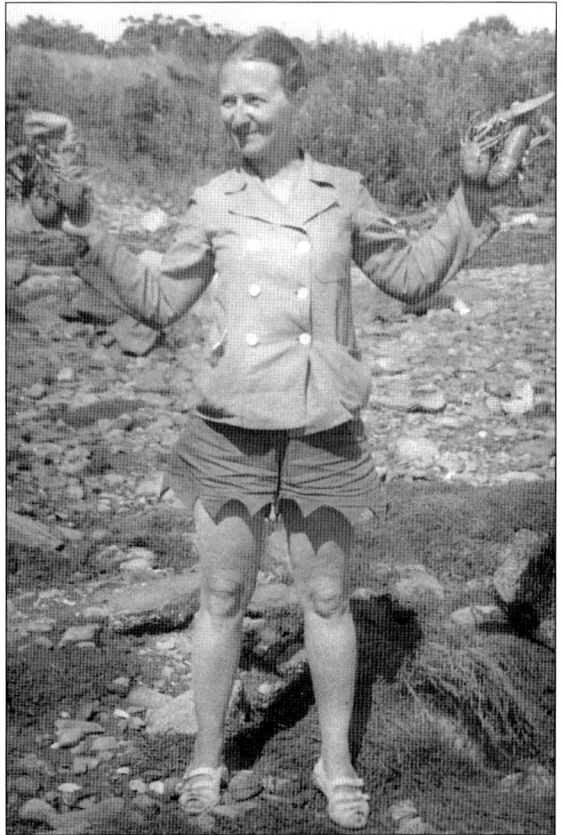

Elizabeth Parks Rupp (1907–1990) has her hands full of lobsters. Maine is defined by its 3,000-mile coastline and the seafood it provides. Fishermen have always trapped lobsters in the waters around Peaks Island, including the Wabanaki people before the Europeans arrived in the 1500s. Elizabeth Rupp, the daughter of John and Emily Trefethen Parks, lived in Kansas for many years but is buried in the Trefethen family cemetery on Peaks Island.

Observation towers on summer cottages were fairly common in the late 1800s. The tower on the Randall family cottage is a particularly dramatic example. The cottage is on A Street, now known as Upper A Street, which is situated on one of the highest points of land on Peaks Island. All of Portland Harbor can be seen from this third-story tower. Fred A. Millett, an amateur photographer who married into the Randall family, took this photograph around 1900. The cottage was built about 1886. The extended Randall family can be seen enjoying the well-furnished porch, while a baby, shaded by a parasol, sits in an elaborate carriage on the lawn.

It is very likely that this photograph of Portland Harbor was taken from the observation tower of the Randall family cottage pictured on the preceding page. A portion of House Island is visible in the middle ground, including the Sterling and Trefethen lobster pounds and fish processing businesses. The harbor is busy with vessels of all kinds. A massive grain elevator looms over the Portland waterfront. Large gardens can be seen in many islanders' backyards. Fred A. Millett, the photographer, lived on Munjoy Hill in Portland and worked as a bookkeeper and accountant but spent summers on Peaks Island through the 1950s.

Despite the rocky soil, houses made entirely of stones are unusual on Peaks Island. Built around 1914 by Boston residents Frederic Whitney and his wife, Anna Whitney, this house was originally known as the Hermitage but is now simply called the Stone House. Located on Lyndon Avenue in the Tolman Heights neighborhood in the center of the island, it is now part of the Illustration Institute's Faison Artist Residency. This photograph was taken in 1987.

The eastern side of the island facing Long Island and the open ocean is traditionally known as "the Back Shore." It is more sparsely developed than other parts of the island and was settled later. This photograph depicts the area near Spar Cove around 1935. (Courtesy of Susan Hanley.)

Tolman Heights is in the center of Peaks Island. It is named after James H. Tolman (1853–1924), whose family owned property in this area from 1882 until 1965. Tolman was an attorney and a municipal court judge in Westbrook, Maine. He rented several cottages to vacationers and drilled a deep artesian well that provided a steady supply of water to that part of the island.

The Henry Parsons homestead is one of the oldest houses on the island. Parsons (1782–1862) was born in Gloucester, Massachusetts, and married Peaks Islander Sarah Sawyer in 1804. He initially built a log cabin but upgraded to this more substantial home around 1822. It was featured in *American Lumberman* magazine in 1922 with the headline "Wood House Withstands Century of Use."

William Henry Trefethen (1844–1926) is on the left, and his grandson Reed Trefethen (b. 1890) is on the right in the striped cap. The man in the center is unidentified. William, a carpenter, lived his whole life on Peaks Island and is credited with building over 70 cottages. Reed was the son of Prince Trefethen (1868–1894), who died after he accidentally shot himself while duck hunting in Casco Bay.

Emily Trefethen (1875–1964) and her dog, Spud, are pictured here. Trefethen married John Kimball Parks (1859–1937) in 1904. Parks was a chemist in a wholesale drugstore in Portland. The family seemed to have split their time between Munjoy Hill in Portland and Peaks Island, where Emily's parents lived.

Jessica "Jessie" Trefethen (1883–1978) was the daughter of William Henry and Elizabeth Mank Trefethen. A painter, she was a professor of art at Oberlin College in Ohio for many years. She was the author of *Trefethen: The Family and the Landing*, published in 1960, which tells the history of her family and the part of Peaks Island they called home. After her retirement, she lived in and owned the Trefethen Homestead, built in 1844, where she was born and raised. The Trefethen Homestead was originally built as a two-family house by her great-grandfather, Henry Trefethen, for his two eldest children, Harriet N. and William S. Trefethen. It still stands as a private home today.

The Summit House was built by William Smith Brackett (1827–1886) around 1857 at the top of the hill on Brackett Avenue. Brackett was a carpenter and worked for the Portland, Saco & Portsmouth Railroad before he built the Summit House, which, by 1861, he ran as a boardinghouse, one of the earliest in Casco Bay. The Summit House attracted many Canadian guests. Brackett married Adeline Preble Harmon (1825–1910) in 1850. Adeline is remembered as a kind woman who helped raise her grandchildren when her daughters died young. Both William and Adeline are buried in Brackett Cemetery.

This well-furnished garden is at a cottage on Crescent Street around 1930. For the many people who lived on Peaks Island during the summer months, spending a lot of time outdoors was a high priority, making porches and gardens very important. The cottage attached to this garden was built around 1899, and in 1924, it was owned by George Franklin Skillings and his wife, Almira, who used it as a seasonal residence. These may be Skillings family members in the photograph.

Jens Christian Pedersen Sr. (1871–1925), his wife, Grace Trefethen Pedersen (1871–1956), and their young family are pictured here in 1907. Jens, an immigrant, was born in Denmark, and Grace was the daughter of William Henry Trefethen of Peaks Island. The children are, from left to right, (first row) baby Samuel, Jens Peder Gosmer, and Jens Christian; (second row) Elizabeth and William Russell.

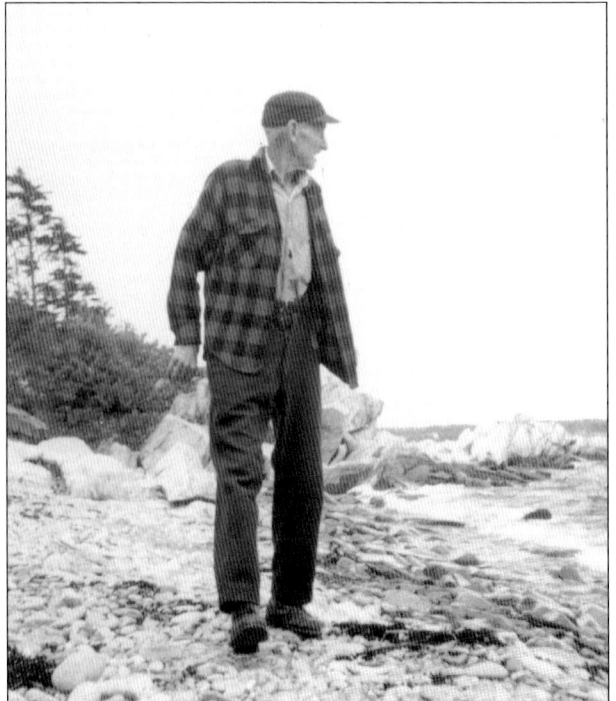

Samuel "Sam" Howe Pedersen (1906–1980) walks on the backshore of Peaks Island in August 1968. Sam is the baby in the photograph above. He was born and died on Peaks Island and is buried in Trefethen Cemetery. He and his brother ran the Peaks Island Garage for almost 40 years. He also drove a taxi and was a lobsterman. He was well-loved and described as the "ultimate gentleman of Peaks Island."

From left to right, John Parks, Chris Pedersen, and Reed Trefethen deer hunt in 1935. The Parks, Pedersen, and Trefethen families were all from Peaks Island and related to one another. Chris Pedersen (1904–1984) ran the Peaks Island Garage with his brother Sam. According to his daughter Reta, he worked seven days a week and rarely left Peaks Island except for a one-week hunting trip each fall. The location of this photograph is unknown, but hunting trips in the Great North Woods of northern Maine were very popular at the time. It is unlikely they were hunting on the island.

These little boys in sailor suits are, from left to right, Harvard Sinclair, Denton Randall, Harold Clark, Elwood Fraser, and Charlie Blackman. Blackman's sister Marie is in the background. They appear to be standing on the wooden boardwalk on Peaks Island that extended over a mile from Forest City Landing to Trefethen's Landing around 1905, when this photograph was taken. The boardwalk was first built in 1899.

Charles O. Blackman (1862–1942) and his wife, Harriet "Hattie" Trefethen Blackman (1861–1964), are pictured at the Blackman Farm around 1930. Charles was a well-known "market gardener" on Peaks Island. Market gardens were small-scale, with produce and flowers being sold directly to consumers and restaurants. With all the hotels and boardinghouses on the island at the time, the Blackmans had many customers. Hattie was over 100 years old when she died.

Livestock such as cattle, ox, sheep, pigs, and poultry was common on Peaks Island through the early 20th century. Islanders were a pretty self-sufficient group. Cows were pastured around the island, including the Evergreen neighborhood, as seen in the photograph from 1926. The woman is unidentified but could be a member of the Scholes family.

Albert Ventres Jr. (1920–2004) poses with his island apiary on October 9, 1947. Albert was the son of Albert S. and Florence Ventres, and he spent much of his life on Peaks Island. Described as "an intelligent, shy man," he lived a reclusive life. A lieutenant, he served as a pilot in the Air Force during World War II. Ventres said he was shot down twice over China during the war. He had a lifelong interest in beekeeping.

Men saw a log with a two-man crosscut saw in this photograph from the Arthur Ross collection. Then, as now, there was high demand for firewood and lumber on Peaks. Like a lot of islanders, Arthur (1893–1958) and his wife, Jennie (1885–1960), did various jobs on the island. Arthur was a sanitation worker, delivered milk, and helped cut ice from island ice ponds in the colder months.

This man may be Arthur Ross around 1930. Snow removal was a huge job in the winter, and a lot of it was done by hand. The chains on the truck tires improved traction on snowy island roads, most of which were unpaved.

This is Capt. George W. Randall (1860–1946) in 1918. He was a well-known fisherman, and like many year-round Peaks Island residents, he profited from the summer visitors to Portland Harbor. A 1907 newspaper article reports, "Captain Randall has been kept busy on these lovely bright days, taking deep sea fishing parties for a half day trip or pleasure seekers in his fine new motor boat the *Tourist*." (Courtesy of Susan Hanley.)

Jack Keoughan and Nancy Randall (1922–2008) are seen on the tennis court at the Trefethen-Evergreen Improvement Association, commonly known as "TEIA" or simply "the Club." It is named after the Trefethen and Evergreen neighborhoods. The tennis and sailing club was a popular place for island youth to hang out. This photograph was taken around 1940.

This tiny cottage near Trefethen's Landing was built around 1884. It was first called Azalea but is now known as Seagull Cottage. In 1963, Seagull Cottage was bequeathed, along with $2,000, to the TEIA by the estate of Emily Trefethen Howe. TEIA owns a clubhouse, built in 1915 as the Dayburn Casino, right next to the cottage. At the time, a "casino" did not simply offer gambling; the Dayburn was a dance hall. Today, the cottage is the summer residence of the TEIA club manager and his family.

Despite the frigid water even in the height of summer, swimming and dock jumping in Portland Harbor have been popular for over a century. Lounging on a float at Trefethen's Landing are a pair of young people, a scene familiar to islanders today. The woman may be Elizabeth Parks (1907–1990), and the young man is unidentified.

This is a smiling Albert Ventres Jr. rowing a skiff off Peaks Island around 1950. Most islanders were comfortable on the water, rowing, fishing, sailing, and working in various maritime trades. Ventres Jr. grew up living on the island.

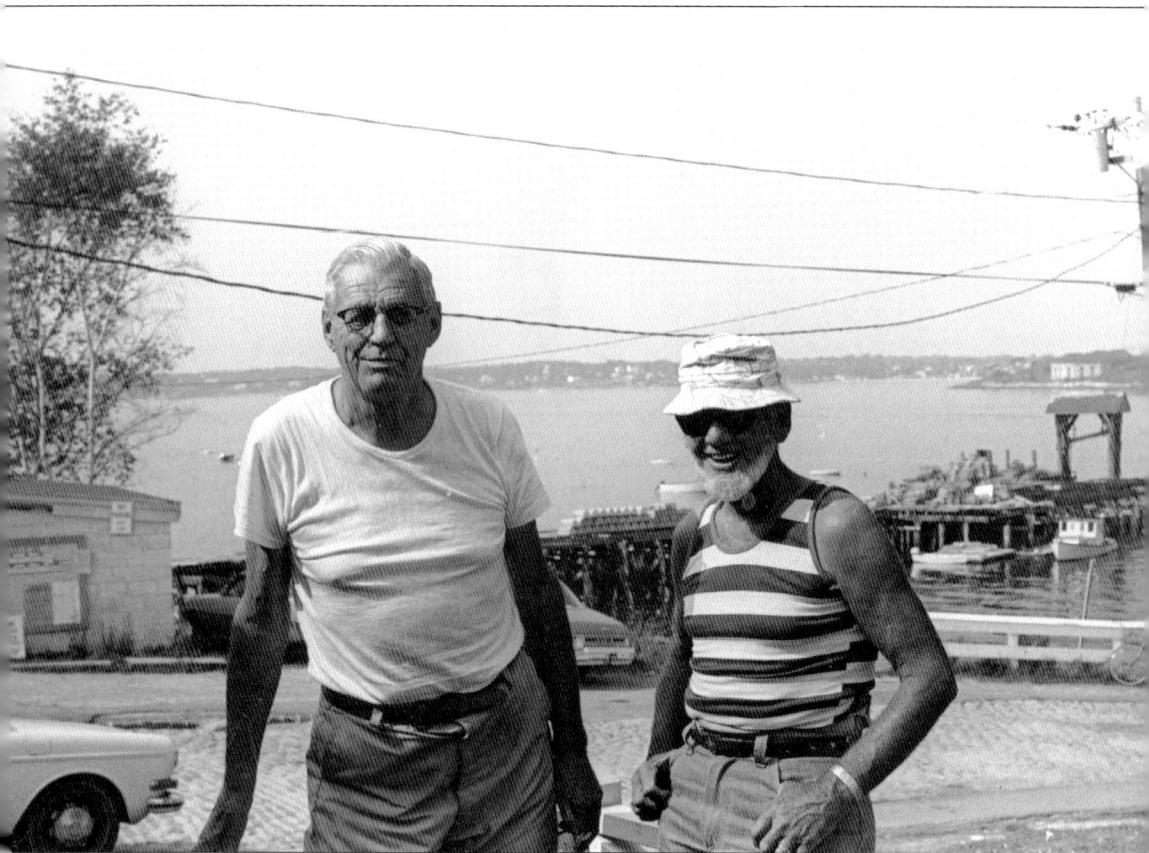

In this image are Bill Greenlaw (left) and Leonard "Lenny" Waugh (right) in the Down Front area of Peaks Island near Forest City Landing. Both men lived on Welch Street, and Waugh drove the taxi for a time. The ramshackle wharf, Jones Landing, can be seen in the background. Jones Landing was one of the earliest working wharves on Peaks Island, but by 1976, when this photograph was taken, it was in serious disrepair. Fort Scammell on House Island is also visible to the right. Fort Scammell was built in 1808 as part of the defenses of Portland Harbor. It was unarmed by 1903.

Three

THE REGIMENTAL BUILDINGS

The Fifth Maine Regiment Memorial Hall and the Eighth Maine Regiment Memorial Lodge are seen across Ryefield Cove on the south shore of Peaks Island around 1892. Civil War veterans from these regiments constructed the buildings to provide a relaxing place to gather in the summer and to meet for annual regimental reunions. The lone "Pair Tree" stands nearby, a local landmark at the time.

Taken around 1890, this is a very early view of the Fifth Maine Regiment Memorial Hall, which was completed in 1888. Cushing Island is visible across Whitehead Passage in the background, with Ram Island peeking out behind it. Long Point, known as Picnic Point today, is on the right. Peaks Island was largely deforested at the time, and many islanders had farms and raised livestock including cattle, sheep, and pigs. Fences, such as the stone and wood types seen here, crisscrossed the island and kept animals mostly contained. Members of the Noyes, King, Bragdon, Chase, Webber, and Pinkham families pose in the foreground.

This photograph of the Fifth Maine Regiment Memorial Hall was taken a year or two after it opened in 1888. Newspaper articles at the time credit Portland architects Francis Fassett and Frederick Tompson with designing the building in the winter of 1887–1888. The architectural form is a hybrid of Queen Anne and Shingle styles.

This view of the Fifth Maine Regiment Memorial Hall was taken between 1888 and 1890, from a boat in Whitehead Passage, the body of water between Peaks and Cushing Islands. This part of the island was sparsely populated at the time, but there were a few neighboring cottages, such as one called Hatetoleaveit, just visible in the background with a tent beside it.

The veterans and members of the Fifth Maine Regiment Association chose Peaks Island for their 18th annual reunion held June 24, 1885, several years before they built their own Memorial Hall. The soldiers and their families pose in front of the Greenwood Garden Bierhaus. Known as the "Fighting Fifth," the 5th Maine Regiment mustered into service in June 1861 and saw three years of hard fighting in every major battle in the Eastern Theater, including Bull Run, Antietam, and

Gettysburg. Of the nearly 1,500 men who served, only around 200 remained to be mustered out in July 1864. The others resigned or were otherwise discharged, died in battle or from disease, were transferred to other units, or were taken prisoner by the Confederates. Some deserted, and others went missing in action.

After hosting reunions at various public places in Portland and Peaks Island, the 5th Maine veterans wanted a home to call their own. The Fifth Maine Regiment Memorial Hall was proposed in the winter of 1887. Funds were raised by selling shares of stock in the building. It was constructed very quickly by James G. Sanborn, who had served as a sergeant in Company H. Capt. Benjamin Norton, another 5th Maine veteran, painted it. The building was dedicated on August 1, 1888, less than a year after plans were drawn up. This photograph depicts the second reunion held in the memorial hall, in the summer of 1889.

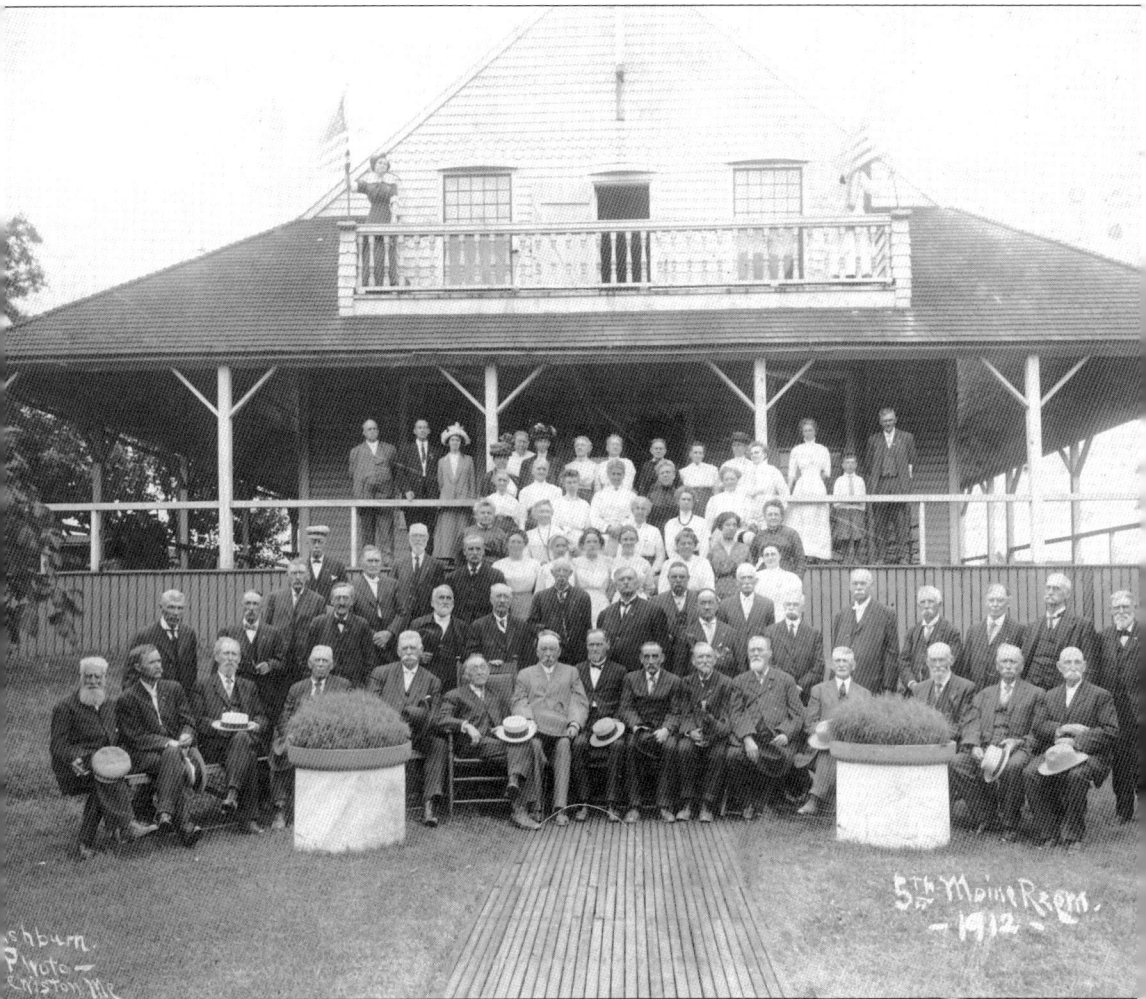

By the 1912 reunion, the number of 5th Maine Regiment veterans who were able to participate had dwindled. Forty-seven years had passed since the end of the Civil War in 1865, and the men were in their 60s, 70s, and 80s. The final reunion was in 1940, when the last 5th Maine veteran died, but their families kept up the tradition for a few more years. The young chestnut tree just visible to the left still shades the lawn today.

The south face of the Fifth Maine Regiment Memorial Hall was originally the formal main entrance to the building. Visitors would walk around the covered wraparound porch and enter through the double doors on the ocean side. On Queen Anne/Shingle buildings, the location of the tower commonly indicates the main facade. The north entrance is what most people use today, but when the hall was occupied by the veterans themselves, that door was probably utilized mainly to move luggage and other supplies in and out of the building. The kitchen extension is visible to the left. Added around 1899, it was removed in the late 1950s.

The Eighth Maine Regiment Memorial Lodge was completed in 1891 as a place for 8th Maine veterans to vacation with their families and gather for annual reunions. Located a few hundred feet away from the Fifth Maine Regiment Memorial Hall, it was also designed by Portland architects Francis Fassett and Frederic Tompson in the Shingle style. Larger than the Fifth Maine building, it was also more expensive, costing about $12,000 to construct. The Fifth Maine cost about $3,000. The Eighth Maine is privately owned by descendants of the original veterans and operates as a seasonal hotel.

Despite the rocks, cold water, and the pronounced lack of sand, this beach below the Eighth Maine Regiment Memorial Lodge was a popular spot for swimming, as seen in this postcard postmarked 1909. The landmark Pair Tree is visible to the left.

This photograph was taken from the top of the Fifth Maine Regiment Memorial Hall observation tower around 1930. The circular tower was accessible by ladder and open to the elements for several decades after the building was dedicated in 1888. At some point in the early 1900s, it was enclosed, maybe for safety reasons. The tower offered a 360-degree view of the surrounding landscape.

The Eighth Maine Regiment Memorial Lodge and the Pair Tree are depicted here around 1905. Beginning in 1893, the Fifth Maine and the Eighth Maine Memorial Associations shared a water well. The windmill in the foreground might have powered the pump that brought the water to the surface. Access to clean and reliable water on Peaks Island was a perennial problem until an underwater main brought water from Sebago Lake to the island in 1920.

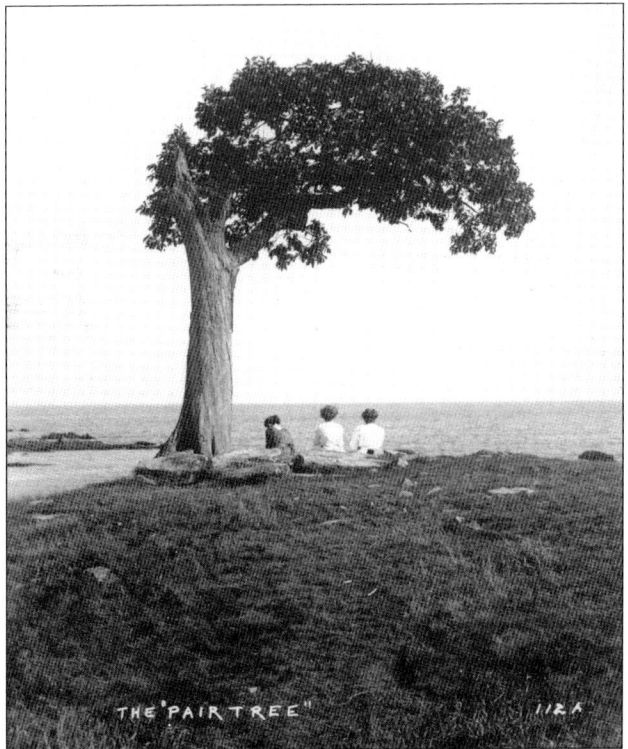

Standing alone near the Eighth Maine, this hearty oak tree was misshapen by the winds whipping off the open ocean. It was a popular place for couples to meet, hence the name Pair Tree. The tree was said to be over 150 years old when it toppled in a wind storm in 1912, which made the newspapers. One article reported, "Mariners have sighted it as a landmark. Millions of people have known and loved it."

Rye Field Cove, Peaks Island, Me.

By 1910, the southern part of Peaks Island had filled with summer cottages clustered near the shore to take advantage of the views across Whitehead Passage. The Fifth Maine Regiment Memorial Hall and the Eighth Maine Regiment Memorial Lodge are visible across Ryefield Cove, as seen from Torrington Point.

FIFTH MAINE BUILDING, PEAKS ISLAND, MAINE

This c. 1935 view of the Fifth Maine was taken near the end of its use by the veterans. The last reunion was held in the building in 1940, and the last overnight guest stayed in 1947. As the veterans passed away, their surviving families struggled to maintain the building. World War II made things even more difficult. The building fell into serious disrepair by the early 1950s.

These two snapshots show the main room in the Fifth Maine Regiment Memorial Hall. Taken in 1939, they show the building right at the end of its active use by the 5th Maine Regiment veterans and their families. The building had a museum-like quality even when it was used for overnight stays and reunions by the regiment members. Many of the framed portraits of the veterans on the walls are in the same places over 80 years later. The glass cases containing battlefield relics collected by the men are also intact today. The cabinet Victrola and piano show that music was important to the visitors.

By the 1970s, the Fifth Maine Regiment Memorial Hall had suffered decades of neglect and was structurally unsound. In 1954, the remaining descendants of the veterans agreed to deed the building over to benefit the Peaks Island community, with stipulations that ensured it would always memorialize the 5th Maine Regiment. Efforts to preserve the building faltered until 1977, when restoration work began in earnest. In the photograph above, Steven Walsh and Sean O'Gane weatherproof the porch so work could continue throughout the long winter. These men were participants in the Comprehensive Employment and Training Act (CETA) program. The federal program offered work in nonprofit organizations to long-term unemployed people as well as summer jobs to high school students.

Caring for a historic building located a few feet from the ocean has its challenges. The salt air takes a toll on wood, paint, and metal. Maintenance is a continuous process, and when one project ends, another begins. In this photograph from the early 1990s, an unidentified man perilously works on the Fifth Maine's tower roof. The roof was replaced once again in 2019.

The hefty oval boulder, its surface relatively smooth aside from the modest inscription "Fifth Maine Volunteers 1861–1865," is visible in the lower left of this photograph. This is the Memorial Boulder, and it has been on the lawn of the Fifth Maine building since 1908. Said to weigh 10 tons, it took 14 horses to move it from one end of the island to the lawn of the Fifth Maine, where it is today. This gathering may have commemorated Casco Bay Islands Day on August 19, 1962.

Rev. Theodore "Ted" Warren (1935–2021) served as the president of the reinvigorated Fifth Maine Regiment Museum in the 1980s. A history teacher at Portland High School, he was part of a team of dedicated Peaks Islanders who worked very hard in those years to restore the building to its former glory. He is shown here with a newly installed marker from Greater Portland Landmarks designating the building a site of historic interest. He and fellow islander Bea Chapman, shown examining a Civil War uniform, assumed leadership roles in the organization and worked side by side to raise awareness and guide the Fifth Maine to a place of stability.

The Fifth Maine Regiment Community Center, as it was then known, is pictured around 1978. The circular planters had been in place since at least 1912, as they are visible in the reunion photograph taken that year. At some point, the Memorial Boulder was moved closer to the road. The chestnut tree, a tiny sapling in 1912, now towers over the building. Very little else about the building has changed.

Four

THE CONEY ISLAND PERIOD

The Gem Theater dominates the skyline at Forest City Landing. This 1913 image also shows the location of the carbide gas plant (building with a tall smokestack on the right) that burned coal to produce gas for the Forest City area of Peaks Island. The Peaks Island Corporation was formed in 1922 to bring widespread electric lights to Peaks Island.

Forest City Landing is seen from an approaching ferryboat. This photograph, captured by Fred Millet, was taken in 1915 or later since the building to the left of the Gem Theater was not present on a detailed 1914 map of the island. The windmill seen rising above the trees was used to pump a well. Most of the buildings in this image did not survive the fires of 1934 and 1936.

By 1915, theater was a well-established tradition on Peaks Island. Theater managers invited actors from big cities like New York or Washington, DC, to work on the island for the summer. Actors enjoyed the break from city life and island visitors enjoyed the high-quality productions. This photograph, autographed by two actors of the time, is written to Bill Leavitt, owner of the shooting gallery on the Peaks Island boardwalk.

A large beach just below the Gem Theater attracted families seeking cool summer breezes and healthy salt air. Swimming was not uncommon, although most people visited the beach in street clothes. For those who felt like a spontaneous dip, "swimming costumes" were available to rent. Islanders capitalized on the tourist trade, leaving no opportunity behind. (Courtesy of Susan Hanley.)

Restaurants and lunchrooms began to pop up on Peaks Island during the 1880s when day trips to the island became popular. "Shore dinners" featuring fish chowder and lobster were popular options, easily provided by local fishing families. The Forest City Lunch Room and Picnic Stand was one of the early restaurants on the island.

This 1906 tintype came from the Peaks Island Studio, located along the boardwalk. By 1906, the tintype was something of a carnival novelty, having been replaced by paper-based photographs. Indeed, Peaks Island tourists could choose between having their image appear on tin or paper. Tintype exposures could take up to two minutes, which is why people often appeared stiff. These two young men seem quite relaxed by tintype standards. (Courtesy of Susan Hanley.)

Gem Theatre and Peaks Island House, Peaks Island, Me.

This view shows Island Avenue in front of the Gem Theater and the New Peaks Island House. The New Peaks Island House had 100 rooms when it opened in 1904, replacing the first, much smaller Peaks Island House that only accommodated 60 guests. The dirt path that ends on the corner of Welch Street and Island Avenue was well-used by cottagers and was known as Elephant Avenue.

This 1913 letter, written on letterhead that clearly states, "Hebrew patronage not desired," reveals the discriminatory practices of the management at the New Peaks Island House and Annexes. This type of discrimination persisted into the 1950s, when nearly two-thirds of Maine's resorts refused to accept Jewish guests, the highest percentage of any state in the union. (Courtesy of Susan Hanley.)

The New Peaks Island
House and Annexes

Peaks Island, Me. RALPH E. ROWE
MANAGER

HEBREW PATRONAGE NOT DESIRED

Peaks Island, Me.,
June 7, 1913.

Miss Mary R. Chandler,

Columbia Falls, Maine.

My Dear Miss Chandler:

Your esteemed favor of June 6th is at hand.
Have reserved room as requested, and feel confident that we can please you.

Assuring you that we shall make every effort
to make your stay enjoyable, I am,

Very truly yours,

R. E. Rowe,

RER-CH

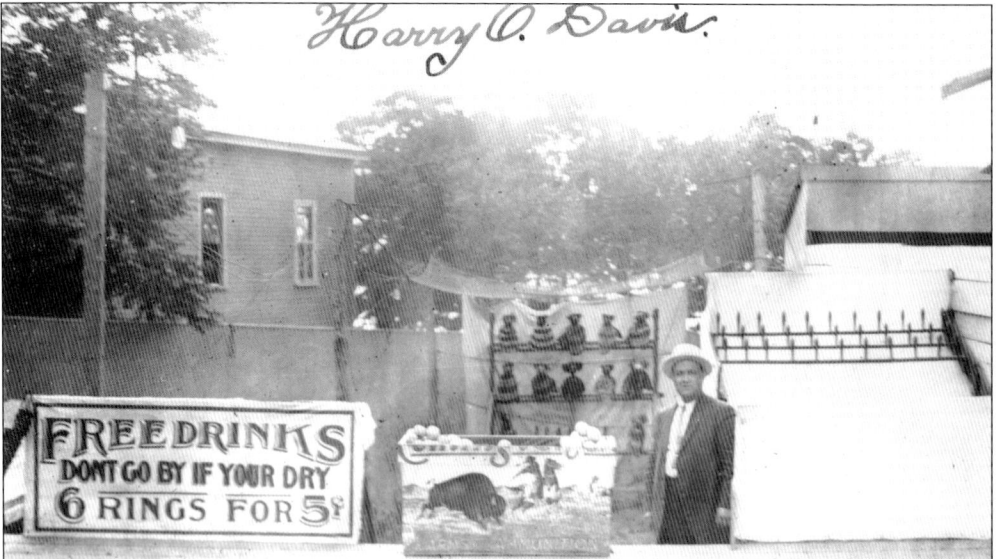

Harry O. Davis.

FREE DRINKS
DON'T GO BY IF YOUR DRY
6 RINGS FOR 5¢

Peaks Island Maine Season 1916

In the early 1900s, Peaks Island lived up to its nickname, the "Coney Island of Maine," with its host of summer entertainments, including theaters, dining halls, roller skating, bowling, and amusements that lined the boardwalk between Forest City Landing and Greenwood Garden. The barker at this ring toss game pulled in passersby with the promise of a free drink and a prize.

DEVELOPING AND PRINTING DONE HERE

HAVE YOUR PICTURE ON A POSTAL CARD 3 FOR 25¢

Before personal box cameras like George Eastman's Brownie became popular in the 1920s, having one's picture taken and printed on a postcard was a true novelty. Postcards were extremely popular in the early 1900s and cost just a penny to mail. The shop window also displays scenic black and white images that tourists could take home as souvenirs of their visit to the island.

Besides promising fun and prizes, the owner of this stand pulled customers into his shooting gallery by appealing to their patriotism. Shooting was so popular that Peaks Island had more than one shooting gallery in 1915, although inviting beginners to learn to shoot on the crowded boardwalk seems a bit dangerous according to modern sensibilities.

Islanders developed novel "dime attractions" that provided visitors with a bit of fun and gave Forest City Landing a slightly honky-tonk reputation. This image seems to place the Giggle Show inside the tall stockade fence that surrounded Greenwood Garden. Perhaps these straight-faced men found the variety show a hard sell since guests had already paid a 25¢ entrance fee at the Greenwood Garden gate.

THE INNES HOUSE. PEAKS ISLAND, ME.

The Innes House was one of the longest-running hotels on Peaks Island. It began its life in the 1850s as the Casco House, overlooking Portland Harbor, where Adams Street is today. In 1880, Sarah Innes moved the hotel closer to Island Avenue, and in 1881, it was moved again to the corner of Welch Street and Island Avenue, where the building still sits today. (Courtesy of Susan Hanley.)

PEAKS ISLAND, ME.   A popular house at Trefethens.   164

Just a few months after Robert and Harriet Skillings built Oak Cottage in 1865, they began taking in boarders, a common practice on the island. An 1891 advertisement lists capacity as 20 guests, each paying $1.50 a day or $8–10 a week. Many islanders, who otherwise fished or farmed, happily provided room and board to seasonal visitors to earn extra money. Oak Cottage still stands on Pleasant Avenue above the former Trefethen's Landing. (Courtesy of Susan Hanley.)

The hotel at Trefethen's Landing was originally named the Montreal House. It was built, owned, and operated by William S. Trefethen in the 1850s. He later expanded and renamed it the Valley View House. After he died in 1907, the property was sold, and it burned to the ground on July 6, 1909. Luckily, "the season" had not peaked, so the one guest in the hotel made it out safely.

The Valley View House, situated where the TEIA tennis courts are today, remained a very popular hotel for over 50 years. In this image from the 1880s, several guests have paused their croquet game for a photograph. Croquet, skating, and bowling were considered "ladylike" sports at the time, all of which were offered by island establishments. Young Jessie Trefethen is seated in the first row, second from left.

Brochures from Ye Headland Inn touted it as "the only hotel on the ocean side of Peaks Island" and then assured guests that homelike comforts and an air of refinement and culture would make them feel less like hotel guests and more like "members of a large house party." The inn also had its own gas plant, water system, indoor plumbing, and fine cuisine—"well cooked and served daintily."

The Knickerbocker Hotel, built in 1903, sat high above Evergreen Landing and provided patrons with sweeping views of Casco Bay. It escaped the fire of 1918 that consumed its two-story addition and eight nearby cottages but was not so lucky in 1925. In February of that year, the Knickerbocker burned down.

Hotel guests at the Knickerbocker enjoyed the fresh air, pine woods, and sea views that surrounded Evergreen Landing. It was the "quiet" side of the island. Evenings included musicales, poetry recitations, or card parties. When the Dayburn Casino opened at Trefethen Landing in 1915, dancing was available. And for those who craved a crowd, a trip down to Forest City Landing filled the bill. (Courtesy of Susan Hanley.)

During the 1880s, the Avenue House was one of the island's grand hotels with suites of rooms, a dining hall, and an attached music and dance hall. By the 1930s, it had lost some of its grandeur and operated as a rooming house. In 1985, Portland's zoning board approved the conversion of the property to condos, which are still in existence today.

Robert T. Sterling opened the Oceanic House in 1875, situated on a grassy hill overlooking Trefethen's Landing. Catherine Sterling took over when her husband died unexpectedly just a year later. She ran the Oceanic until 1913, advertising as far as New York and Philadelphia. In 1949, the Oceanic House burned down leaving the wide-open space between Pleasant Avenue and Island Avenue that can still be seen today.

Five

COMMUNITY LIFE

PEAKS ISLAND SCHOOL   SEVENTH AND EIGHTH GRADE PUPILS   1948.

In 1948, only 12 students graduated from the Peaks Island School to continue their education "up town" at Portland High School. Their departure was not enough to relieve the overcrowding at the island school. By 1950, enrollment swelled to 275 students, and city council appropriated $4,500 to buy and renovate the old phone company building on Island Avenue to house 30 incoming kindergartners. The school also instituted a "staggered start" to relieve crowding.

Rapid population growth between 1850 and 1870 more than doubled the number of children in school and led to parental complaints about overcrowding. In 1869, a visiting school committee found 82 students in the one-room schoolhouse, and the city agreed to build a new school. The one-story building seen in this 1895 photograph remains the heart of the island's school today.

Since it was built in 1869, the island's school has undergone several renovations. A second story was added in the late 1800s, and indoor bathrooms were added in 1915. This picture from 1964 clearly shows the classroom wing added in 1945 (on the right) and the gym that was added in 1958 (on the left).

The Peaks Island School was particularly full of students during the 1950s and 1960s. The school offered a wide variety of activities beyond reading, writing, and arithmetic. Shown here are the school basketball team (above) and the cheerleading squad (below) around 1963. School activities included chorus, newspaper, yearbook, both varsity and intramural basketball, volleyball, Explorer's Club, the Variety Show, Library Club, and cheerleading. Classrooms had class librarians and air-raid wardens. Many students also played musical instruments. The abandoned buildings on the military reservation were untamed playgrounds for youngsters then, just as they are now. The schoolyard was also a source of fun—and treasure. In November 1954, one student found a 1749 British copper coin buried in the dirt. Just a week later, another student found an 1858 penny in almost the same spot.

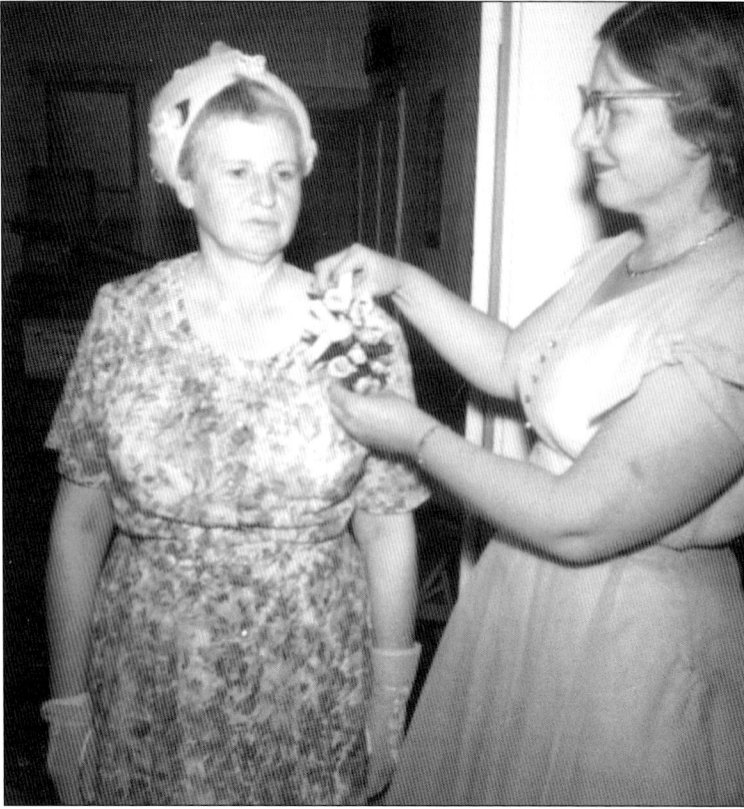

Beatrice Thompson was a fourth-grade teacher at the Peaks Island School for 30 years before her retirement; she is shown here receiving a corsage at her retirement party. She worked alongside another beloved teacher, Virginia Brackett, who taught fifth graders at the school for 30 years as well. Both women were island residents who had a long-lasting, positive influence on the youth of Peaks Island.

The Peaks Island Calends Study Club was founded in 1928 and active for 50 years. The club is seen here enjoying a picnic at Pine Point in Scarborough, Maine, in June 1941. Members took turns hosting the club in their homes and leading discussions about issues that affected home, community, and country. Topics ranged from "Architecture for the Future" to "What's Your Favorite Christmas Custom" to "What Change Would You Like to See?"

Boy Scout Troop 20 was active on Peaks Island in the 1940s, conducting paper drives, holding monthly pack meetings, and earning merit badges. This photograph hints at the fact that during the war years, Boy Scout uniforms may have been an added expense that some families chose to avoid. Uniformed or not, these Scouts learned skills like knot tying and camping. At one pack meeting in 1947, each den presented a sketch on the theme "The World of Tomorrow." The audience enjoyed watching the boys portray men from Mars, travel in a rocket ship, and deliver a television broadcast from the future. Later that same year, five Peaks Island Scouts were awarded special honors: Ronald W. Scribner, new Scout and tenderfoot award; Donald M. Higgins, second class award; Walter Beesley, merit badge in home repair, carpentry, and woodworking; Allan Ward, merit badge in lifesaving; and Richard Briggs, merit badge in first aid.

Peaks Island Girl Scout Troop 179 was founded in 1955. In this c. 1959 photograph, troop leader Eadle Dambrie (center of the second row) proudly stands with her Scouts. Pictured here are, from left to right, (first row, seated) Alexina Feeney, Sharon Douglas, Barbara Van Ness, Diane Hambleton, Catherine Mulkern, and Angela Dambrie; (second row, standing) Stephanie Dambrie, Barbara Briggs, Bonnie MacVane, Eadle Dambrie, and three unidentified persons.

These Girls Scouts are ready to join the Memorial Day Parade in 1972. Both Boy Scout and Girl Scout troops have traditionally been part of Peaks Island's parades. The girl on the left is wearing a Cadette uniform, for girls grades six through eight. The other girls are Junior Girl Scouts, grades four and five.

The boys' softball team leads the Fourth of July parade as it makes its way down Island Avenue sometime in the 1930s, passing the Atlantic & Pacific Tea Company building on the corner of Island Avenue and Welch Street (where the Down Front Ice Cream Shop is currently located). (Courtesy of Susan Hanley.)

Four Peaks Island Scout troops assemble in the island parking lot to participate in the Memorial Day parade in 1964: the Girl Scouts, the Brownies, the Boy Scouts, and the Cub Scouts. Even today, Peaks Island Memorial Day parades traditionally begin with a service at the dock, then march down Island and Central Avenues, and end with a memorial service at Pond Grove Cemetery. The Army dock can be seen on the left.

The young men of the Peaks Island Baseball Club pose together in August 1904. Island teams vied for bragging rights in a fiercely competitive summer league. The back of the photograph notes that the team was "formed by R.T. Sterling." This most likely refers to Robert Thayer Sterling, who was born on Peaks Island in 1876 and went on to become a keeper at Portland Headlight from 1928 to 1946.

By the 1950s, Little League Baseball was popular with island boys. This photograph shows Harry Golden, born in 1946, practicing his batting stance. Golden attended the Peaks Island school for his entire grammar school education and won the 12th annual *Sunday Telegram* spelling bee as an eighth grader. His winning word was "respectively."

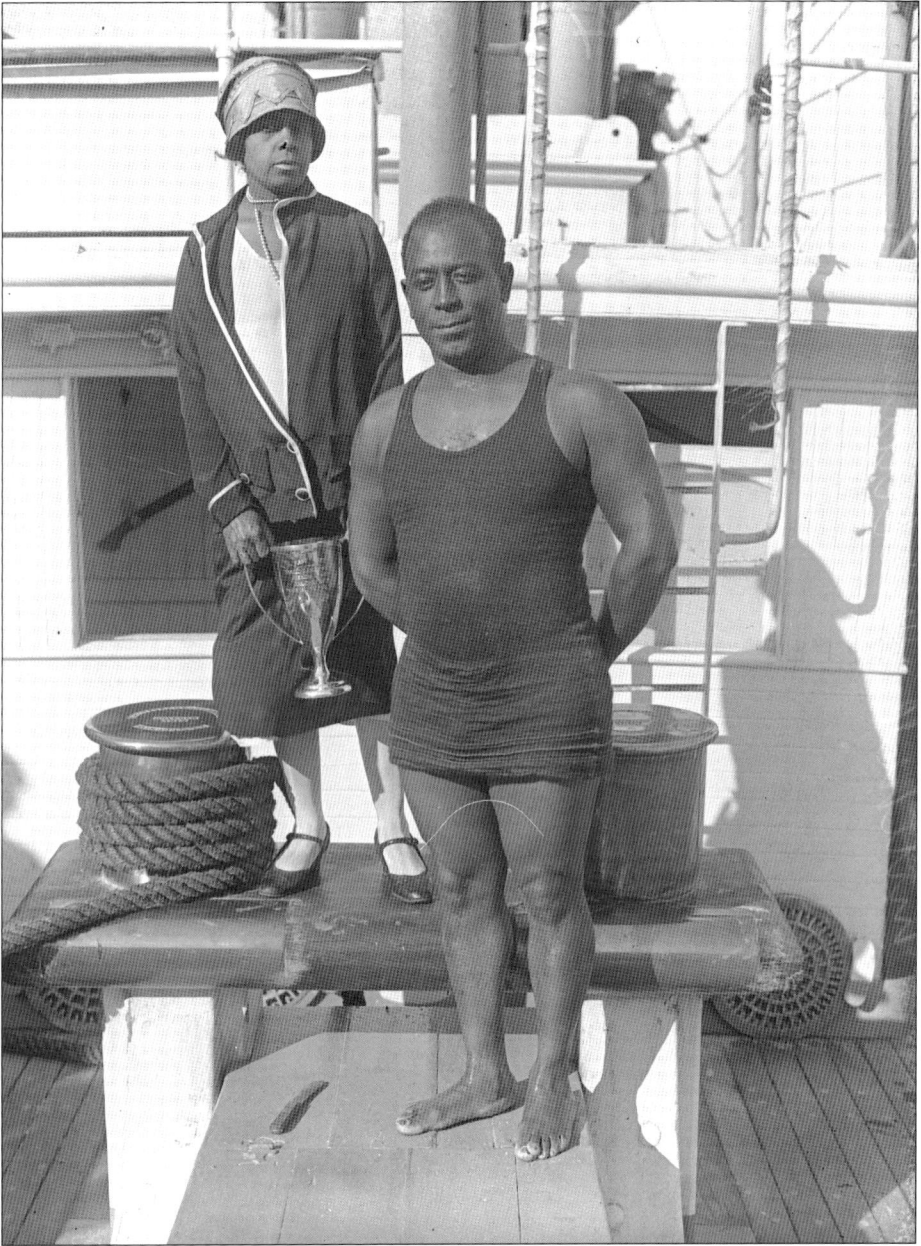

Mitchell Williams, a Portland native, won the 1927 Portland to Peaks swim. Williams is seen here in his bathing suit on the deck of a steamboat. His wife, Florence "Flossie" Eastman Williams, also a Portland native, stands behind him. Mitchell graduated from Tuskegee Institute, but like so many at the time, the family struggled during the Depression. The Williamses owned a few acres in Scarborough, Maine, and ran it as a small farm during the summers to grow vegetables and raise animals for the family larder. They returned to their home on Anderson Street in Portland so their seven children could attend school. No record exists of Mitchell swimming in other Portland to Peaks races, held annually except during World War II when the harbor was being used by the military. The swim race started back up again after its wartime hiatus and is still run today. (Courtesy of the Maine Historical Society/MaineToday Media.)

These young men are ready for a tennis match on the early, rugged tennis courts of the Trefethen-Evergreen Improvement Association. TEIA installed its first tennis courts in 1930, hoping to attract more members to the organization. At the time, tennis was one of the few sports that was acceptable for both men and women.

TEIA was founded in 1912 and began meeting on the second floor of Webber's Store in 1913. In 1922, the group bought the Dayburn Casino for $3,600 to use as its clubhouse. Membership grew quickly to 423 members in 1925, but by 1947, there were just 100. In spite of declining membership, the Trefethen Beach, where this Sunday school picnic was held in 1946, remained popular with the community.

TEIA was conceived as a neighborhood improvement association, and in its early days, the organization spearheaded civic projects that did, indeed, improve the life of islanders in the Trefethen and Evergreen areas. The association oversaw the conversion of gas streetlights to electric, paid for the construction of a sidewalk between Trefethen and Evergreen landings, created a humane society for stray dogs, and lobbied for better ferry service, new sewers, improved fire protection, and well-maintained roads. The energy of the club members seemed boundless. Social activities included all the popular entertainments of the time: speakers, musicals, plays, dancers, magic shows, and vaudeville acts. The Davies sisters, Mabel and Mary, who were instrumental in the foundation of the club, gave lectures about birds seen in the bird sanctuary they created on their property. In this 1926 photograph, families enjoy an outing to the "Festival of Nations" put on by club members, including a visit to the small Swiss chalet specially constructed for the event.

SUNDAY MORNING AT ST. CHRISTOPHER'S
PEAKS ISLAND, MAINE

Catholic services came to Peaks Island in 1911 when Mass began being celebrated at the Greenwood Garden Dance Pavilion. Mass was also held in the Gem Theater for a period until the growing number of Catholics on the island warranted a dedicated Catholic church. In June 1923, negotiations were set in motion to purchase the Littlejohn property at the corner of Island and Central Avenues. The 30,000-square-foot property included an eight-room house that was used as the church rectory. Construction began in October 1923, and St. Christopher Church was completed in March 1924 at a cost of $35,000. In the 1950s, a large stained-glass window was installed in the apse wall, the gift of island residents William and Mary O'Keefe. In this 1930 image, parishioners pour out of St. Christopher Church as Mass ends. Note that Central Avenue is not paved. (Courtesy of Susan Hanley.)

The Sisters of Notre Dame came to Peaks Island in 1967 to establish a year-round convent and summer retreat for nuns. This picture in 1968 shows, from left to right, Sister Rosina, Sister Marie Noel, and Sister Ann St. Joseph. Missing from the picture is Sister Margaret Catherine who was transferred after being accused of purchasing an island home in her own name, against the rules of the church, to establish a nursing home on Peaks. Her removal upset many islanders, who defended her.

St. Joseph by the Sea convent thrived during the 1980s. A note on this June 1983 photograph says, "Picture with our associate Theresa Swain at a party here." However, by 1995, the convent closed, and three monks established a monastery on the property. They intended to support themselves by brewing beer. Though savvy marketers—their label claimed "Beer is proof that God loves and wants us to be happy"—they gave up after one batch.

The church that would one day become the Brackett Memorial Church began as the Methodist Episcopal Church in 1861. At that time, there were just 30 homes on Peaks Island, and the church the islanders built was simple. A 1902 bequest from the Henry M. Brackett estate enlarged the building, which was renamed Brackett Memorial Church. The vestry (attached and to the right of the main church) was built in 1902, and the Fellowship Hall (not yet built in this picture) was added in 1958.

Even in today's more secular world, churches play a central role in Peaks Island life, providing members with spiritual, social, and emotional support. This photograph from the 1940s shows the combined Brackett Memorial Church Choir and the Brackett Memorial Junior Choir in their choir robes.

Kitchen bands were popular across the country in the 1930s and early 1940s, often included as part of local variety shows. This photograph of the Peaks Island Sink-a-Pater band appears to be taken in front of the stage at Brackett Memorial Church. As the name implies, "instruments" are actually kitchen implements such as rolling pins, graters, flour sifters, washboards, tea kettles, and saucepan lids. Homemade marching band uniforms were topped with chef's hats to complete the kitchen reference. The woman at the far left holding a small accordion is Beatrice "Bea" Hill. Hill was also very active in the Ladies Auxiliary of the American Legion Randall MacVane Post 142.

TILLERS OF THE SOIL 1942.

Kitty Grant, seen on the right of this photograph in a black dress, was best known locally for her play *Rosemary of the Island*, which she wrote and directed. The play was performed at Brackett Memorial Church for many years, and although no script exists, the playbill indicates that the play is about events at the church itself, since the cast of characters includes the janitor of the church, the organist, and members of the choir (among other characters). By 1942, Grant authored a new play called *Tillers of the Soil*. Many of the same actors appeared in her new play, this time dressed as pioneers. Neither script nor playbill exists for this play, but props and costumes suggest that it is a story about frontier living. In the early 1900s, Kitty Grant directed shows at many of the island theaters, including the Gem Theater. The musical variety shows were headlined "Kitty Grant's Lady Minstrels," although men also appeared in the productions.

Actors from the play *Rosemary of the Island* pose outside Brackett Memorial Church for professional photographs that were available for the audience to buy during the play's intermission. These images are likely from the 1939 rendition of the play. Note the stained-glass flower in the church window that is still there today.

PHOTO BY B.V.BICKNELL

THE GREENWOOD PLAYERS, PEAKS ISLAND, ME.

The Greenwood Playhouse operated as a summer stock theater. Martin Landau, lying on the grass to the left of this image, made his stage debut on Peaks Island in 1951. Fifty years later, he recalled, "We did 12 shows in 13 weeks. It was great but it was tough." Although summer stock has stopped, the stage has not gone dark. A community variety show is now in its 72nd year and counting.

The original Webber's store, shown here in the early 1900s, was a stable bought by Arthur F. Webber from Capt. William S. Trefethen in 1912. The building was beside the fruit orchard planted around the Valley View House. It was later enlarged to become Webber's Market with a separate post office, a mainstay of the Trefethen neighborhood. That market was later run by Don and Clio Webber until they retired in 1976.

Harvey Trefethen operated an icehouse on the east side of Peaks Island, known simply as the "ice pond" today. He cut ice during the winter and stored it in a large three-to-four-story wooden building for delivery in the summer months. During the 1920s, before refrigerators became commonplace, there were three separate ice ponds and ice delivery services on Peaks Island.

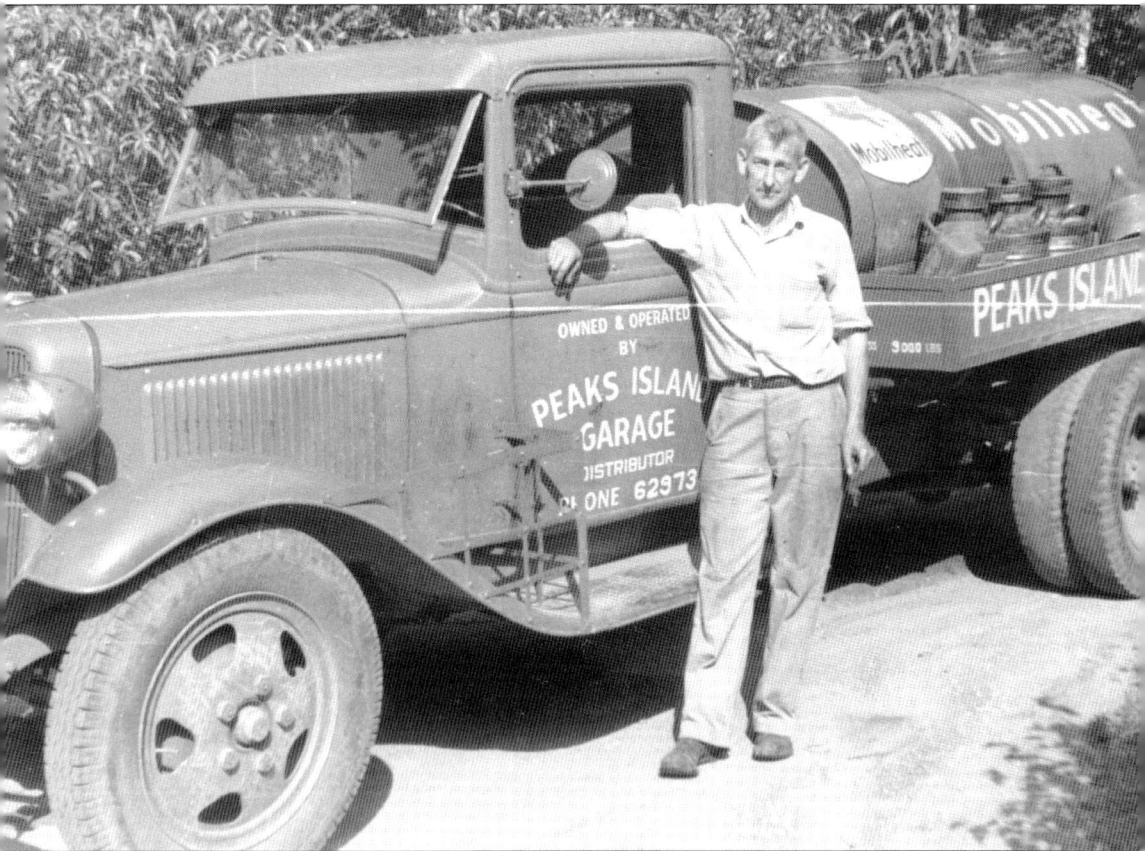

Sam Pedersen (seen here beside his oil delivery truck) and his brother Chris Pedersen owned the Peaks Island Garage for 38 years. The garage evolved from a "hired car" business they took over when their older brother Bill went to college. Portland required taxis to have meters, so the brothers circumvented the regulations by offering hired cars rather than taxis. As the garage grew, Sam and Chris added a gas station, repaired vehicles, and delivered heating oil and kerosene. The garage burned in 1968. The black smoke from burning fuel oil could be seen from Portland. The now empty lot north of Plante's laundromat and gas station on Island Avenue is the original site of the garage.

Before cars were prevalent on Peaks Island, many businesses had home deliveries, such as bakeries, icemen, and grocery stores. This Oakhurst Dairy truck is from the 1930s, but the Oakhurst milkman remained a fixture of Peaks Island life until the early 1970s.

Providing visitors with transportation has been a source of island employment since the late 1800s, when horse-drawn carriages moved people and luggage between the landings and the grand hotels. In the 1920s, taxis lined Welch Street waiting to pick up passengers as they disembarked. This photograph from 1978 is labeled "Taxi with Charlie the driver."

Peaks Island has had a fire station since 1884, although access to water to fight fires in the island's interior has always been a problem. Residents have lobbied for improved fire protection in the form of fire trucks, hydrants, and a firefighting force since 1889. This 1964 image demonstrates the fruits of their efforts: a fire station with two pumper trucks and a dedicated fireman.

Farragut Cottage, Peaks Island.

Greetings from Portland, Maine.

Farragut Cottage, seen on this postcard, became the home of Peaks Island's American Legion Post 142. Actor John Ford, who summered on Peaks Island, helped establish the island's American Legion in 1937 with two donations (totaling $800) toward the purchase and repair of the cottage. He wrote in a note with one of the donations, "Every time I smell a fish boat . . . it reminds me of Joe Trott's motor boat and my heart goes homeward." (Courtesy of Susan Hanley.)

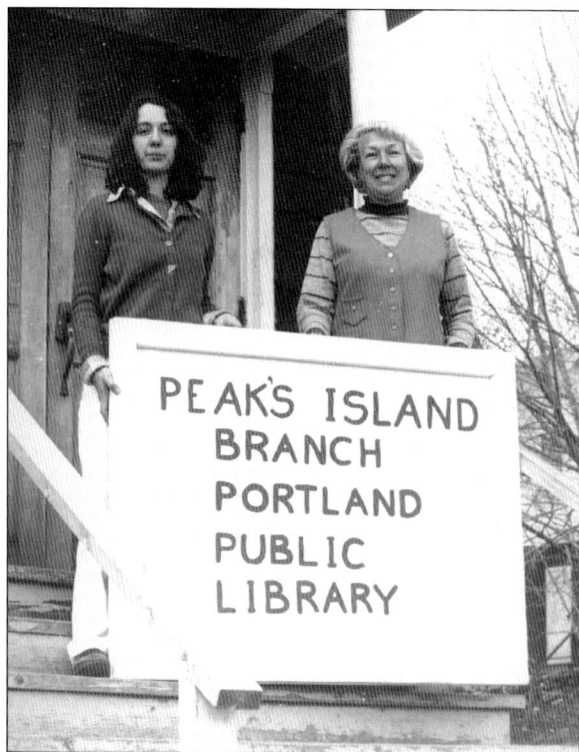

PEAK'S ISLAND BRANCH PORTLAND PUBLIC LIBRARY

The Peaks Island branch of the Portland Public Library opened in the American Legion building on February 5, 1978, with great enthusiasm. Volunteers helped staff the library so that it was open five days a week, between eight and eleven hours per day, plus Saturday mornings. Louise Hutt (left) and Ruth Sargent were two of the first three staff members.

Snow shovelers in 1922 exemplify the community spirit of Peaks Island. These volunteers came together to clear the sidewalks and streets after a heavy snow. In this picture, they are standing on a snow pile in front of the Island Hall (also known as the Forest City Grange) on Island Avenue, before it was taken down in 1959.

The Casco Bay Health Center was dedicated on August 20, 1976. Longtime island resident and nurse practitioner Marge Erico provided residents with on-island health care between twice-weekly visits by Dr. Robert Caven. The building returned to a private home when the health center moved to the Fay Garman House in 2005.

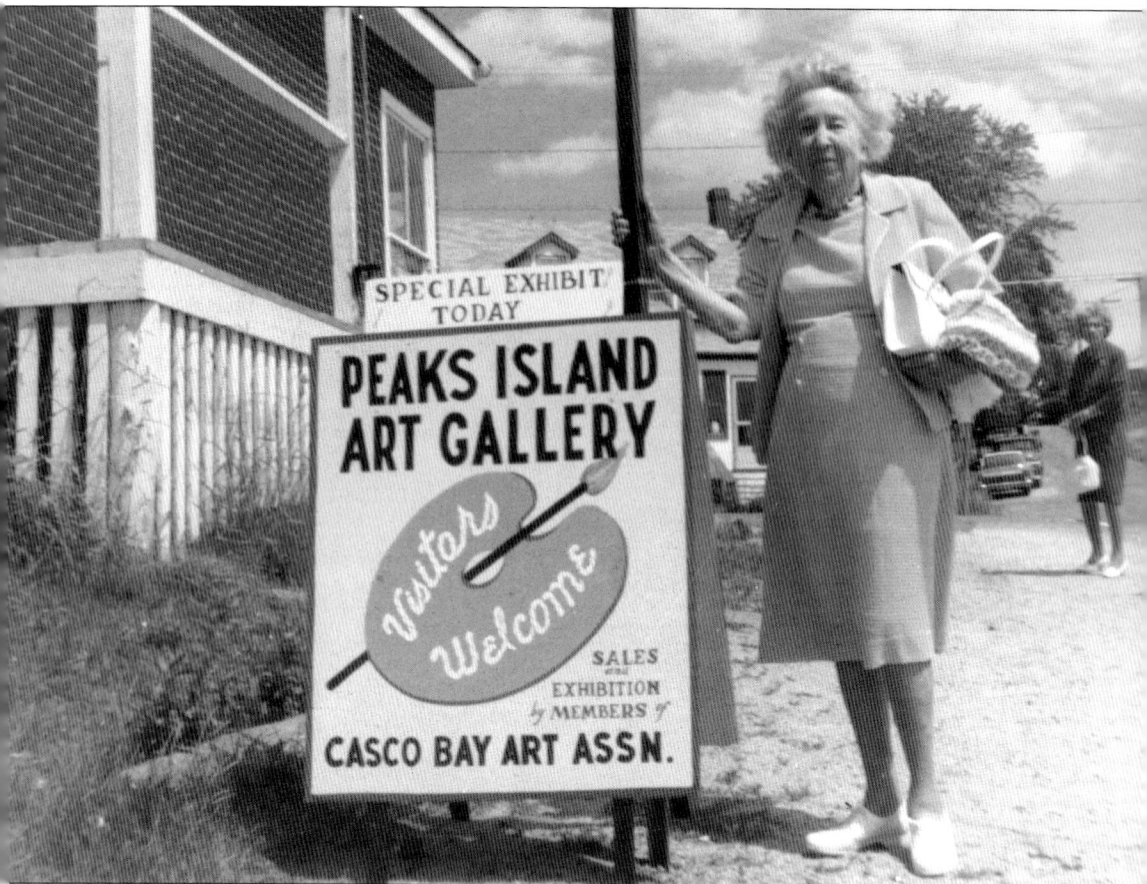

Jessie Trefethen was born and raised on Peaks Island. She was interested in art all her life and pursued an art degree from Mount Holyoke College, then toured Europe on a Cresson Scholarship. She later moved to Ohio to become a professor of art at Oberlin College. When she retired and moved back to Peaks Island, she was instrumental in launching the Casco Bay Art Association. She is seen here on the sidewalk on Welch Street in front of the art gallery that she helped create and where she often exhibited her watercolors of the island's rocky shore. With her nurturing, the community of artists on Peaks Island grew, and the island is still home to many artists today.

Six

WORLD WAR II

PEAKS ISLAND SCHOOL JUNE 5, 1945
PRESENTATION OF MINUTE MAN FLAG AND DEDICATION OF AMBULANCE & JEEP
PHOTO BY DOE

Civilians supported the war effort during World War II in many ways. Students at the Peaks Island School were awarded this Minuteman flag from the US Treasury Department in 1945, recognizing that at least 90 percent of the students were regularly buying war stamps or war bonds.

Battery Steele was built in 1942 as part of the World War II military fortifications in Casco Bay. Pits at the corner of Brackett and Florida Avenues as well as at the corner of Ledgewood and Boulder Roads were created when the military used the soil to camouflage the huge concrete structure with dirt and vegetation. Note the man next to the gun for scale.

Battery Steele was established to target enemy battleships and submarines in Casco Bay. Coordinates from lookout towers and bunkers on Peaks, Cushing, Jewell, and Bailey Islands were radioed into the battery, where they were then triangulated to determine firing positions. In this photograph, Sgt. Angelo Cantalupo is in the battery's self-contained power plant.

Battery Steele's two 16-inch guns could fire a 2,000-pound shot 26 miles out to sea. Each gun was 60 feet long and weighed approximately 50 tons. Although the guns were never fired in battle, they were test-fired once at about three-quarters full charge, reportedly causing vibrations that broke window panes in several island homes. This c. 1946 image shows one of the gun casemates.

Battery Steele's long, central corridor connected its two guns. Rooms to either side of the main corridor held shells, powder, and other supplies. The battery had its own power supply: three diesel engines that generated the electricity needed to run the equipment. This c. 1946 picture shows the shell room.

This World War II lookout tower as well as a few smaller bunkers still exist on Peaks Island today. Portland Harbor was a strategic target, home of a Liberty Ship shipyard, a Navy fuel depot, and the launchpad for the Atlantic fleet. Submarine nets, mines, and underwater detectors prevented German U-boats from entering Casco Bay. Despite all efforts, a German submarine sank the USS *Eagle PE-56* just south of Portland on April 23, 1945—just two weeks before Germany surrendered.

The military constructed 58 separate structures on Peaks Island during the war, including these wooden buildings inside the reservation. The reservation had its own network of water pipes. The fire hydrant, seen in front of the fire station to the right of this image, was no match for the huge fire in 1957 that swept across the east side of Peaks Island, burning most of the buildings on the military reservation.

These soldiers appear relaxed and confident in the summer of 1946 after the war was over. At its height, the military reservation housed approximately 800 men and was spread across 198 acres that had been taken from islanders by eminent domain. During the war, 190 men manned Battery Steele, and 123 men manned the smaller Battery Cravens. The entire military reservation, including its shoreline, was off-limits to the 700 residents who lived on Peaks Island at the time. Barbed-wire fencing surrounded the reservation, and sentries manned the entry gates. However, there were opportunities for civilians and military personnel to meet. When off-duty, soldiers were allowed to leave the base and patronize the island stores, bars, and eateries. Pictured here are, from left to right, (first row) Pvt. John Newton and Pvt. Leonard Murray; (second row) Sgt. Fred Baumgardner; (third row) Capt. Larry Cutshaw and Pfc. Ralph Boling; (fourth row) Pfc. Laurence Blutcher.

Military ships fill Portland Harbor, dwarfing the passenger ferry that is sailing toward Forest City Landing on the right. The wharf in the left of the picture was owned by the military. Called the Army dock, it was built on the protected harbor side of the island. All the supplies used to construct the military reservation were landed at this wharf and driven overland during the two-year building project.

Peaks Islanders' view of Whitehead Passage and Cushing Island was only slightly altered during the war years. Cushing Island was home to Fort Levett, which was built during the Spanish-American War and also used during both world wars. Here, a lookout bunker can be seen above the cliffs as well as a radar tower that is cleverly disguised as a water tower.

Seen here is the graduating class from the First Sergeants School on the Peaks Island Military Reservation in 1943. The third man from the left in the second row is Sgt. John J. Sapp, who served in Battery E of the Harbor Defense of Portland, the battery that was in charge of the 16-inch guns at Battery Steele. A short time after World War II ended, the Army decided that fixed harbor defenses such as Battery Steele were not effective against new military technology like long-range missiles and nuclear weapons. The military reservation on Peaks Island was declared surplus property. The two guns at Battery Steele, which had cost nearly $1 million to make, were removed, cut up with blowtorches, and sold as scrap metal for $15,000 in 1948. After the raging fire of 1957, the military eventually sold the property, once valued at $2.3 million, for just $40,000 in 1958.

After the war ended, life on the military reservation was not as restrictive. In this 1946 image, Sgt. Angelo Cantalupo and island resident Eunice Randall pose together for a photograph. Both photography and civilians were forbidden on the military reservation during the height of the war. The military presence impacted islanders' lives in many ways. Islanders who lived on land taken by the military lost their homes and livelihoods. Lobstermen and fishermen had to work inside Portland Harbor once submarine nets closed off access to Casco Bay, and fishing in the harbor was challenging. Harbor traffic was busy, and the water was covered with an oily film due to the many large ships in the harbor. Civilians had to install blackout curtains on their windows, streetlights were turned off, and cars could not use their headlights at night—rules enforced by civilian air raid patrol (ARP) wardens. One positive aspect of having the military on Peaks Island was the economic boost. The military injected money into the local economy and created support jobs for civilians.

Peaks Islander Margaret Randall served during World War II as a recruiting officer for the Women's Army Corps (WAC). After the war, she became a teacher. She retired to Peaks Island, where she volunteered at the Fifth Maine Regiment Community Center, the Brackett Memorial Church, and the Randall-MacVane Post of the American Legion, named after her brother Earle MacNeill Randall, who was killed during training maneuvers in 1922.

Peaks Islander Tom Quigg (in front) and friends sit atop one of the two six-inch guns at Battery Cravens. The guns had a range of 15 miles and could shoot up to five rounds per minute, which was much faster than the guns at Battery Steele. The large structure directly behind the men is a thick shield that the gun crew stood inside to protect themselves from enemy fire.

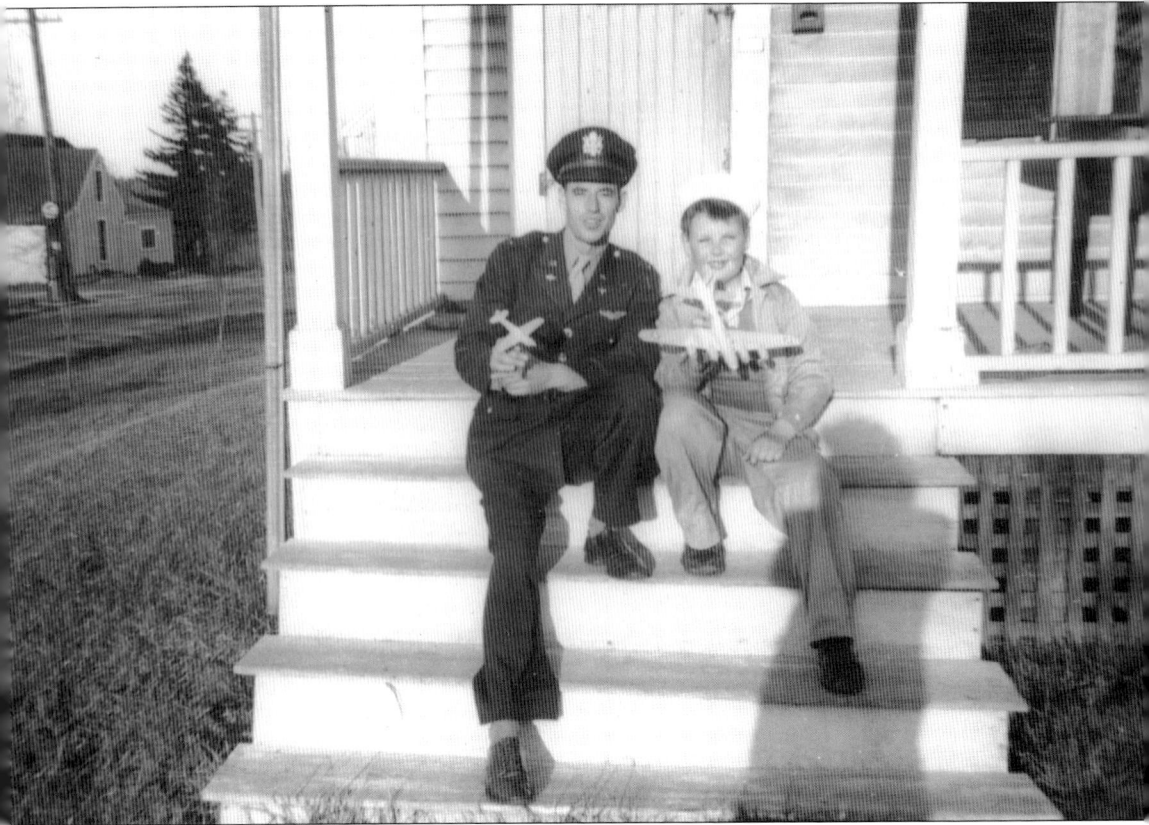

In this photograph, taken in April 1945 on the front steps of the Ventres home on Pleasant Avenue, Albert Ventres (in uniform) and Walter Beesley each hold a handmade model airplane built by Beesley. Ventres affectionately titled this photograph "Air Minded Men" and noted that Beesley is holding a B-17 Flying Fortress and he is holding a P-40 Warhawk.

Seven

MARITIME LIFE AND PORTLAND HARBOR

Portland Harbor is Peaks Island's front yard. This c. 1900 view of the harbor and House Island was taken by Fred Millett from the tower of his family cottage on Peaks Island (see page 38). Fort Scammell, on the left, was built in 1808 as part of a seacoast fortification system. House Island has a long history in the fishing industry. The Trefethen family operated a wholesale lobster business there. Their wharves are visible to the right.

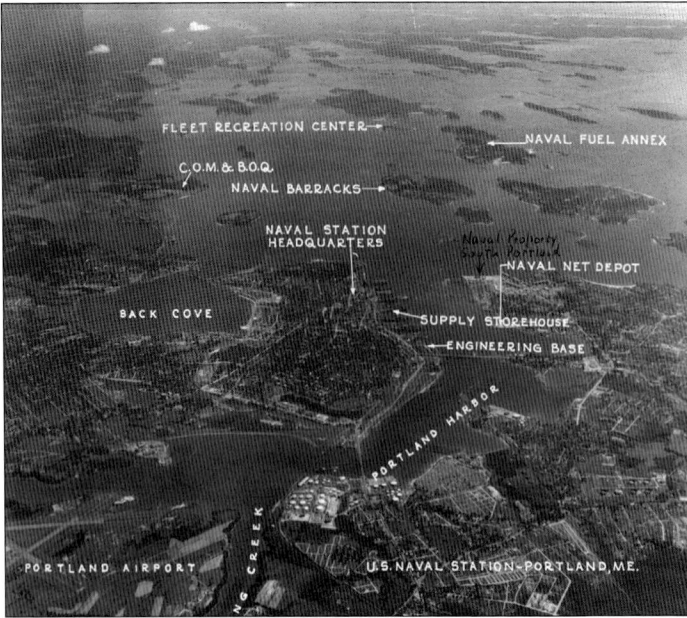

This aerial view of Portland Harbor naval installations was taken in July 1947, shortly after the end of World War II. Both the US Army and Navy had a huge presence in Portland Harbor during that war. There were military forts and related reservations all over Casco Bay because it offered protected anchorage close to North Atlantic convoy routes. The harbor was crowded with a density of maritime traffic that is hard to imagine today. (Courtesy of the National Archives at Boston.)

This is known as a Virginia-class battleship, likely the USS *Georgia* (BB-15), which was built at Bath Iron Works in Bath, Maine. The ship visited Portland Harbor soon after it was launched in 1904. The Virginia-class battleships were built for the US Navy in the early 1900s, after the United States' victory in the Spanish-American War, which demonstrated the need for ships suited for operations abroad.

The ferry *Conanicut*, built in 1886, worked in Rhode Island waters. For decades, it ferried people to and from Conanicut Island in Narragansett Bay. In the late 1920s, it was sold and brought to Portland Harbor for use as a passenger ferry for the Casco Bay islands. It languished unused and was broken up for scrap by a maritime wrecking company on the Portland waterfront around 1930. By the end of their useful lives, the component parts of ships were often worth more than if they were functioning, much like old cars today.

This "spark plug" lighthouse was built in Portland Harbor in 1897 to mark the dangerous Spring Point Ledge, where many ships had run aground. It also had a fog bell that sounded every 12 seconds. In 1951, a 900-foot granite breakwater was added to connect the lighthouse to the mainland, but for over 50 years, it looked like this. It was added to the National Register of Historic Places in 1988 and opened to the public in 1999.

The Portland waterfront remained a busy place after World War II. This postcard image was taken in the late 1940s, and a wide variety of vessels are pictured: small lobster boats, large trawlers, and a wooden steam tugboat called *Portland*, built in 1902 for the Central Wharf Towboat Company. By 1950, the tug had moved to Yarmouth, Maine, and was used as a floating restaurant. (Courtesy of Susan Hanley.)

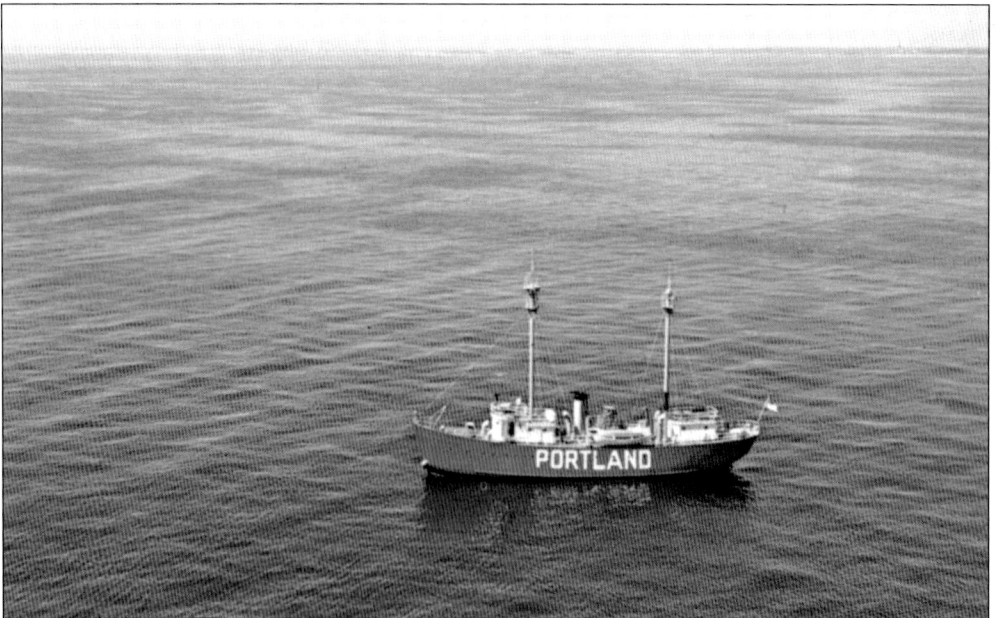

The lightship *Portland* anchored at the entrance to Portland Harbor in the 1960s. Lightships were moored in places dangerous to navigation and equipped with warning lights and fog bells. They were essentially floating lighthouses. By the mid-1970s, the Coast Guard had replaced most lightships with large navigational buoys.

State and federal laws require that a pilot familiar with the area safely guide large ships in and out of Portland Harbor. The *Portland Pilot* was built at Union Wharf in Portland in 1931 and served as a pilot boat in the harbor until 1969. She was converted into a schooner as part of the Maine "windjammer" tourist fleet. She sailed from Rockport, Maine, in 1969 and then to Belfast, Maine, in 2015. She was purchased by the Portland Schooner Company in 2018 and returned to Portland as the *Timberwind*. The boat was listed in the National Register of Historic Places in 1992.

In the 1910s and 1920s, there was an unusual tradition of women having their photographs taken posing on bell buoys floating in the ocean. This unidentified woman may have been a member or a friend of the Trefethen family. Even more unusual is her outfit, which appears to be a full-length dress, rather than a bathing costume.

The USS Missouri is one of the most famous battleships in US history and is best remembered as the site of the surrender of the Empire of Japan, which ended World War II. The ship visited Portland Harbor on June 29, 1946, and Peaks Islanders Mary Ventres and her mother, Florence, took a tour, posing on the prow of the historic ship with the massive triple gun turrets visible behind them.

Casco Bay Lines is one of the oldest ferry services in the United States and provides regular, year-round passenger service to several islands in Casco Bay, including Peaks. Shipping freight to and from the islands is a lesser-known, but no less important, service. Everything that cannot be carried by hand or moved in a cart has to be freighted, including essentials like firewood, household appliances, furniture, and lumber. In this c. 1965 photograph, Casco Bay Lines was located on Custom House Wharf. It relocated to the Maine State Pier in 1988. (Courtesy of Susan Hanley.)

Pumpkin Knob is a tiny, two-acre, heavily wooded island just off the northern tip of Peaks Island in Hussey Sound. The house just visible in this c. 1900 photograph is no longer standing. Privately owned, the island has changed hands many times over the years, and today, it boasts a small cottage, a gazebo, a dock, and reportedly, a lot of poison ivy.

INDEX

ABOUT THE FIFTH MAINE MUSEUM

The Fifth Maine Regiment Memorial Hall was built in 1888 by the veterans of the 5th Maine Volunteer Regiment as a memorial and reunion hall. The veterans created a quiet, almost sacred space where they gathered, reminisced, and drew comfort from each other. As time passed, the reunions grew smaller and smaller (the last one was in 1940), and the building fell into disrepair.

In 1956, the Fifth Maine Regiment building was given to the Peaks Island community by the descendants of the veterans who constructed it. Since then, restoration work has brought the building back to its former glory. It is an architectural gem that is now in the National Register of Historic Places.

Today, the building houses the Fifth Maine Museum, a museum that tells two intriguing and related stories through objects, artifacts, and exhibits: the story of the Civil War's 5th Maine Volunteer Regiment and the history of Peaks Island, from its early settlement to its days as the "Coney Island of the North" to its role during World War II and beyond. The Fifth Maine Museum is also an active community center, hosting dozens of community events each year for local nonprofits and organizations. A large wraparound porch, spacious interior, and stunning ocean views make the Fifth Maine Museum a perfect setting for weddings, private parties, professional workshops, and music concerts.

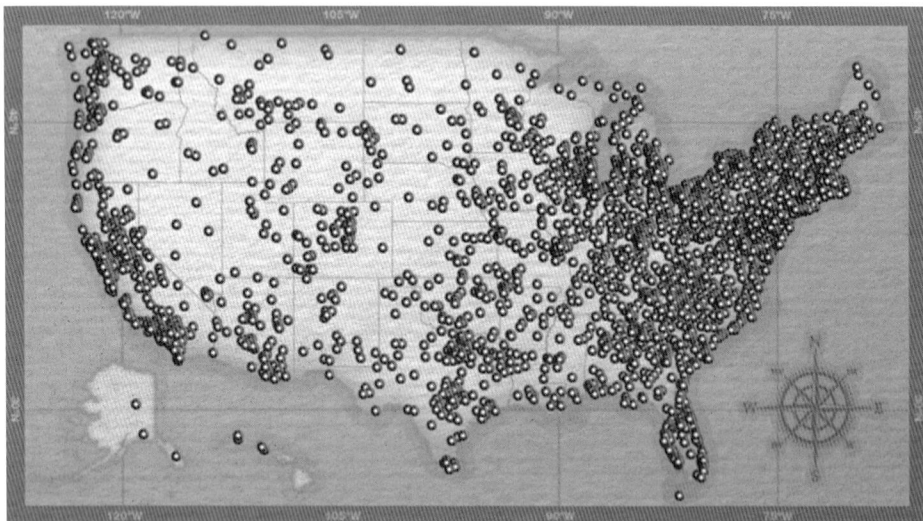